Have You Heard The One About... Religion

✦

Lucy Blackman

iUniverse, Inc.
Bloomington

Have You Heard The One About... Religion

iUniverse books may be ordered through booksellers or by contacting:

iUniverse
1663 Liberty Drive
Bloomington, IN 47403
www.iuniverse.com
1-800-Authors (1-800-288-4677)

Because of the dynamic nature of the Internet, any web addresses or links contained in this book may have changed since publication and may no longer be valid. The views expressed in this work are solely those of the author and do not necessarily reflect the views of the publisher, and the publisher hereby disclaims any responsibility for them.

Any people depicted in stock imagery provided by Thinkstock are models, and such images are being used for illustrative purposes only.

Certain stock imagery © Thinkstock.

ISBN: 978-1-4620-3343-0 (sc)
ISBN: 978-1-4620-3344-7 (ebk)

Printed in the United States of America

iUniverse rev. date: 08/02/2011

Four Catholic ladies are having coffee together discussing how important their children are.

The first one tells her friends, "My son is a priest. When he walks in a room, everyone calls him 'Father'."

The second Catholic woman chirps, "Well, my son is a bishop. Whenever he walks into a room, people say, 'Your Grace'."

The third Catholic woman says smugly, "Well, not to put you down, but my son is a cardinal. Whenever he walks into a room, people say 'Your Eminence'."

The fourth Catholic woman sips her coffee in silence. The first three women give her this subtle "Well...?"

She replies, "My son is a gorgeous, 6'2", hard-bodied, well-hung, male stripper. Whenever he walks into a room, women say "My God!"

*   *   *

Nun Chips

An elderly nun who was living in a convent next to a construction site noticed the coarse language of the workers and felt she should spend some time with them to correct their ways.

She decided she would take her lunch, sit with the workers and talk with them for a while. So she put her small sandwich in a brown bag and walked over to the spot where the men were eating.

As she approached the group, she said, with a big smile, "Do you men know Jesus Christ?" They shook their heads and looked at each other. Then one of the workers looked up into the steelwork and yelled, "Anybody up there know Jesus Christ?"

One of the steelworkers yelled down, "Yeah! Why?" The worker yelled back, "His wife's here with his lunch!"

*   *   *

Church Bulletin

At the evening service tonight, the sermon topic will be "What is Hell?" come early and listen to our choir practice.

*   *   *

Dear Lord,

So far today, God, I've done all right. I haven't gossiped, haven't lost my temper, haven't been greedy, grumpy, nasty, selfish, or even indulgent.

I'm very thankful for that — but in a very short time, God, I'm going to get out of bed, and from that moment on, I'm going to need a lot of help!

Amen.

*   *   *

Behaving Badly

One day God was looking down at Earth and saw all of the inappropriate behavior that was going on. He decided to send an angel down to Earth to check it out. When the angel returned, he told God, "Yes, it is bad on Earth; 95% are misbehaving and 5% are not."

God thought for a moment and said, "Maybe I had better send down a second angel to get another opinion." So God called another angel and sent him to Earth for a time.

When that angel returned he went to God and said, "Yes, it's true. The Earth is in decline; 95% are misbehaving and 5% are being good."

God was not pleased. So while he was debating what to do about the 95%, He decided to e-mail the 5% that were good to encourage them — give them a little something to help them keep going.

Do you know what that e-mail said?

I didn't get one either!

*   *   *

Church Bulletin

The church will host an evening of fine dining, super entertainment and gracious hostility.

*   *   *

The Confession

A parish priest was being honored at a dinner on the twenty-fifth anniversary of his arrival in that parish. A leading local politician, who was a member of the congregation, was chosen to make the presentation and give a little speech at the dinner, but he was delayed in traffic, so the priest decided to say his own few words while they waited.

"You will understand," he said, "The seal of the confessional can never be broken. However, I got my first impressions of the parish from the first confession I heard here. I can only hint vaguely about this, but when I came here twenty-five years ago, I thought I had been assigned to a terrible place.

The very first chap who entered my confessional told me how he had stolen a television set, and when stopped by the police, had almost murdered the officer. Further, he told me he had stolen money from his parents, embezzled money from his place of business, had an affair with his boss's wife, taken illegal drugs, and gave VD to his sister.

I was appalled. But as the days went on, I knew that my people were not all like that, and I had, indeed, come to a fine parish full of understanding and loving people."

Just as the priest finished his talk, the politician arrived, full of apologies at being late. He immediately began to make the presentation and give his talk. "I'll never forget the first day our parish priest arrived in this parish," said the politician. "In fact, I had the honor of being the first one to go to him in confession."

Moral: DON'T EVER BE LATE!

*   *   *

I had been teaching my three-year-old daughter, Caitlin, the Lord's Prayer for several evenings at bedtime. She would repeat after me the lines from the prayer. Finally she decided to go solo.

I listened with pride as she carefully enunciated each word right up to the end of the prayer: "Lead us not into temptation," she prayed, "but deliver us some E-Mail."

*　　　*　　　*

A priest and a rabbi had worked in the same neighborhood for years and decided to travel on the train to a non-sectarian conference together.

They got talking and the priest says to the rabbi, "In your faith, you're not supposed to eat ham; have you ever tried it?"

The rabbi, a little embarrassed, said "Yes." The priest asks, "How did you like it?" The rabbi replies, "It was good." The Rabbi then asks the priest, "Have you ever had a woman?" The priest was incensed.

The rabbi says, "I told you my secret; you have to tell me your secret." The priest finally admits he has had a woman. The rabbi says, "Beats ham, doesn't it?"

*　　　*　　　*

An Irish Working Girl

An Irish girl went to London to work as a secretary and began sending home money and gifts to her parents. After a few years they asked her to come home for a visit, as her father was getting frail and elderly.

She pulled up to the family home in a Rolls Royce and stepped out wearing fur and diamonds.

As she walked into the house, her father said "Hmmm, they seem to be paying secretaries awfully well in London." The girl took his hands and said "Dad, I've been meaning to tell you something for years but I didn't want to put it in a letter. I can't hide it from you any longer.

I've become a prostitute." Her father gasped, put his hand on his heart and keeled over. The doctor was called but the old man had clearly lost the will to live. He was put to bed and the priest was called.

As the priest began to administer Extreme Unction, with the mother and daughter weeping and wailing, the old man mutter weakly, "I'm a goner — killed by me own daughter! Killed by the shame of what you've become!"

"Please forgive me," his daughter sobbed, "I only wanted to have nice things. I wanted to be able to send you money and the only way I could do it was by becoming a prostitute."

Brushing the priest aside, the old man sat bolt upright in bed, smiling. "Did you say prostitute? I thought you said Protestant!"

*   *   *

Gumpisms

The day finally arrived: Forrest Gump dies and goes to Heaven. He is at the Pearly Gates, met by St. Peter himself. However, the gates are closed and Forrest approaches the Gatekeeper.

St. Peter says, "Well, Forrest, it's certainly good to see you. We have heard a lot about you. I must inform you that the place is filling up fast, and we've been administering an entrance examination for everyone. The tests are short, but you have to pass them before you can get into Heaven."

Forrest responds, "It shor is good to be here, St. Peter, sir. But nobody ever tolt me about any entrance exam. Shor hope the test ain't too hard; life was a big enough test as it was."

St. Peter goes on, "Yes, I know, Forrest, but the test is only three questions. Here is the first one: What days of the week begin with the letter T? Second: How many seconds are there in a year? Third: What is God's first name?"

Forrest leaves to think the questions over. He returns the next day and sees St. Peter, who waves him up and says, "Now that you have had a chance to think the questions over, tell me your answers."

Forrest says, "Well, the first one — how many days in the week begin with the letter "T"? Shucks, that one's easy. That'd be Today and Tomorrow."

The Saint's eyes open wide and he exclaims, "Forrest, that's not what I was thinking, but ... you do have a point, and I guess I didn't specify, so I'll give you credit for that answer. How about the next one?" asks St. Peter.

"How many seconds in a year?" "Now that one's harder," says

Forrest, "but I thunk and thunk about that and I guess the only answer can be twelve."

Astounded, St. Peter says, "Twelve? Twelve? Forrest, how in Heaven's name could you come up with twelve seconds in a year?"

Forrest says, "Shucks, there's gotta be twelve: January 2nd, February 2nd, March 2nd…"

"Hold it," interrupts St. Peter. "I see where you're going with this, and I see your point, though that wasn't quite what I had in mind, but I'll have to give you credit for that one, too. Let's go on with the next and final question. Can you tell me God's first name?"

"Sure" Forrest replied, "it's Andy."

"Andy?!" exclaimed an exasperated and frustrated St. Peter. "Okay, I can understand how you came up with your answers to my first two questions, but just how in the world did you come up with the name of Andy as the first name of God?"

"Shucks, that was the easiest one of all," Forrest replied. "I learned it from the song…."ANDY WALKS WITH ME, ANDY TALKS WITH ME, ANDY TELLS ME I AM HIS OWN."

St. Peter opened the Pearly Gates and said, "Run, Forrest, run."

*   *   *

A Sunday school teacher asked her children, as they were on the way to church service, "And why is it necessary to be quiet in church?" One bright little girl replied, "Because people are sleeping."

*   *   *

The Teacher

One day a 6-year-old girl was sitting in a classroom. The teacher was going to explain evolution to the children. The teacher asked a little boy:

Teacher: Tommy, do you see the tree outside?

Tommy: Yes.

Teacher: Tommy, do you see the grass outside?

Tommy: Yes.

Teacher: Go outside and look up and see if you can see the sky.

Tommy: Okay. (He returned a few minutes later.) Yes, I saw the sky.

Teacher: Did you see God?

Tommy: No.

Teacher: That's my point. We can't see God because he isn't there. He doesn't exist.

A little girl spoke up and wanted to ask the boy some questions. The teacher agreed and the little girl asked the boy:

Little Girl: Tommy, do you see the tree outside?

Tommy: Yes.

Little Girl: Tommy, do you see the grass outside?

Tommy: Yesssss. (getting tired of the questions this time)

Little Girl: Did you see the sky?
Tommy: Yesssss.
Little Girl: Tommy, do you see the teacher?
Tommy: Yes.
Little Girl: Do you see her brain?
Tommy: No.
Little Girl: Then, according to what we were taught today in school, she must not have one!

*   *   *

One particular four-year-old prayed, "And forgive us our trash baskets as we forgive those who put trash in our baskets."

*   *   *

A Catholic priest was going away to Africa to do some missionary work, and was leaving a trainee priest in charge. The only thing the trainee was not too sure about was the confessional box. "Don't worry, " said the old priest, "I'll make you out a list of what penance to give for certain sins, and whenever anyone comes in to confess, you can consult the list."

While the trainee was in charge, a woman came in to confess. "Bless me, father, for I have sinned," she said.

"What is your sin, my child?" asked the trainee priest.

"I kissed a man," replied the woman.

The trainee priest consulted the list. "Say two Hail Mary's at bedtime," he told her.

"But that's not all," said the woman. "You see, we took each other's clothes off."

The trainee priest consulted the list again. "Say four Hail Mary's at bedtime," he told her.

"But that's not all," the woman went on. "You see, we got into bed together."

"Say 10 Hail Mary's at bedtime."

"But that's not all. You see, we had sex."

"Say 20 Hail Mary's at bedtime."

"But that's not all. You see, I gave him a blowjob."

The trainee priest looked up "blowjob" in every possible context on the list; it wasn't there. So the trainee priest had to leave his box and ask one of the choirboys, "What does Father Docherty give for a blowjob?"

To which the chorister replied, "Milk and cookies."

*   *   *

The Pope is taking a shower. Although he is very strict about the celibacy rules, he occasionally feels the need to empty his holy scrotal sacs, and this is one of those occasions.

Just as he shoots his load, he sees a photographer taking a picture of the holy wad flying through the air.

"Hold on a minute", says the Pope. "You can't do that. You'll destroy the reputation of the Church."

"This picture is my lottery win," says the photographer. "I'll be financially secure for life."

So the Pope offers to buy the camera off the photographer, and after lots of negotiation, they eventually arrive at a figure of two million dollars.

The Pope then dries himself off, and heads off with his new camera. He meets his housekeeper, who spots the camera.

"That looks like a really good camera!," she says, "how much did it cost you?"

"Two million dollars, " replies the Pope.

"TWO MILLION DOLLARS!" says the housekeeper, "They must have seen you coming."

*   *   *

Church Bulletin

Remember in prayer the many who are sick of our community.

*   *   *

The Preacher

There was a Preacher whose wife was expecting a baby. The Preacher went to the congregation and asked for a raise. After much consideration and discussion, they passed a rule that whenever the Preacher's family expanded, so would his paycheck.

After five or six children, this started to get expensive and the congregation decided to hold another meeting to discuss the Preacher's pay.

There was much yelling and bickering about how much the Preacher's additional children were costing the church.

Finally the Preacher got up and spoke to the crowd and said:

"HAVING CHILDREN IS AN ACT OF GOD!"

In the back of the room, a little old man stood up. In his frail voice he said, "SNOW AND RAIN ARE ALSO ACTS OF GOD, BUT WHEN WE GET TOO MUCH, WE WEAR RUBBERS!"

*   *   *

A minister was opening his mail one morning. Drawing a single sheet of paper from an envelope, he found written it only one word: "FOOL."

The next Sunday he announced, "I have known many people who have written letters and forgot to sign their names. But this week I received a letter from someone who signed his name and forgot to write the letter!"

*   *   *

Church Bulletin

The Rector will preach his farewell message after which the choir will sing "Break Forth into Joy".

*   *   *

Catholic School Test

Kids were asked questions about the Old and New Testaments. The following statements about the Bible were written by children. They have not been retouched nor corrected. (i.e., incorrect spelling has been left in.)

1. In the first book of the Bible, Guinessis. God got tired of creating the world so he took the sabbath off.

2. Adam and Eve were created from an Apple tree. Noah's wife was called Joan of Ark. Noah built an ark and the animals came on in pears.

3. Lots wife was a pillar of salt during the day, but a ball of fire during the night.

4. The Jews were a proud people and throughout history they had trouble with unsympathetic Genitals.

5. Sampson was a strongman who let himself be led astray by a Jezebel like Delilah.

6. Samson slayed the Philistines with the axe of the Apostles.

7. Moses led the Jews to the Red sea where they made unleavened bread which is bread without any ingredients.

8. The Egyptians were all drowned in the dessert. Afterwards Moses went up to the Mount Cyanide to get the ten amendments.

9. The first commandment was when Eve told Adam to eat the apple.

10. The seventh Commandment is thou shalt not admit adultery.

11. Moses died before he ever reached Canada. Then Joshua led the Hebrews in the battle of Geritol.

12. The greatest miricle in the bible is when Joshua told his son to stand still and he obeyed him.

13. David was a Hebrew kid who was skilled at playing the liar. He found the Finkelsteins, a race of people who lived in bibical times.

*   *   *

Wrong Side of the Bed

Mother Superior was on her way to late morning prayers, when she passed two novices just leaving early morning prayers, on their way to classes. As she passed the young ladies, Mother Superior said, "Good morning, ladies." The novices replied, "Good morning, Mother Superior, may God be with you." But after they had passed, Mother Superior heard one say to the other, "I think she got out of the wrong side of the bed this morning."

This started Mother Superior, but she chose not to pursue the issue. A little further down the hall, Mother Superior passed two of the sisters who had been teaching at the convent for several years. She greeted them with, "Good morning, Sister Martha, Sister Jessica, may God give you wisdom for our students today." "Good morning, Mother Superior. Thank you, and may God be with you." But again, after passing, Mother Superior overheard, "She got out of the wrong side of bed today."

Baffled, she started to wonder if she had spoken harshly, or with an irritated look on her face. She vowed to be more pleasant. Looking down the hall, Mother Superior saw retired Sister Mary approaching, step by step, with her walker. As Sister Mary was rather deaf, Mother Superior had plenty of time to arrange a pleasant smile on her face, before greeting Sister Mary. "Good morning, Sister Mary. I'm so happy to see you up and about. I pray God watches over you today, and grants you a wonderful day."

"Ah, Good morning, Mother Superior, and thank you. I see you got up on the wrong side of bed this morning." Mother Superior was floored! "Sister Mary, what have I done wrong? I have tried to be pleasant, but three times already today, people have said that about me."

Sister Mary stopped her walker, and looked Mother Superior in the face. "Oh, don't take it personal, Mother Superior. It's just that you're wearing Father Murphy's slippers."

*   *   *

Six-year-old Angie and her four-year-old brother Joel were sitting together in church. Joel giggled, sang and talked out loud. Finally, his big sister had had enough. "You're not supposed to talk out loud in church." "Why? Who's going to stop me?" Joel asked. Angie pointed to the back of the church and said, "See those two men standing by the door? They're hushers."

*   *   *

The wise old Mother Superior from County Tipperary was dying. The nuns gathered around her bed trying to make her comfortable. They gave her some warm milk to drink, but she refused it.

Then one nun took the glass back to the kitchen. Remembering a bottle of Irish whisky received as a gift the previous Christmas, she opened it and poured a generous amount into the warm milk. Back at Mother Superior's bed, she held the glass to her lips.

Mother drank a little, then a little more. Before they knew it, she had drunk the whole glass down to the last drop.

"Mother," the nuns asked in earnest, "Please give us some wisdom before you die."

She raised herself up in the bed with a pious look on her face and said, "Don't sell that cow!"

*   *   *

Melvin comes to confession.
"Father, " he said, "forgive me for I have sinned."
The priest asked, "What did you do, my son?"
"I lusted," Melvin replied.
"Tell me about it," the priest said.
Melvin then related his story. "Father, I am a deliveryman for UPS. Yesterday I was making a delivery in the affluent section of the city. When I rang the bell, the door opened and there

stood the most beautiful woman I have ever seen. She had long blonde hair and eyes like emeralds. She was dressed in a sheer dressing gown that showed her perfect figure. And, she asked seductively if I would like to come in."

"And, what did you do, my son?" asked the priest.

"Father, I did not go in the house, but I lusted. Oh, how I lusted!" replied the man.

"Your sin has been forgiven," replied the priest. "You will get your reward in heaven, my son."

"A reward, Father? What do you think my reward might be?" Melvin asked.

The priest replied, "I think a bale of hay would be appropriate, … you dumb ass."

* * *

George Loves the Races

One day he was there betting on the ponies and nearly losing his shirt when he noticed a priest who stepped out onto the track and blessed the forehead of one of the horses lining up for the fourth race. Lo and behold, this horse — a very long shot — won the race.

George was most interested to see what the priest did in the next race.

Sure enough, he watched the priest step out onto the track as the horses for the fifth race lined up, and placed his blessing on the forehead of one of the horses. George made a beeline for the window and placed a small bet on the horse. Again, even though another long shot, the horse the priest had blessed won the race.

George collected his winnings and anxiously waited to see which horse the priest bestowed his blessing on for the sixth race. The priest stepped out, blessed a horse, George bet on it, and won! George was elated.

As the day went on, the priest continued blessing one of the horses, and it always came in first. George began to pull in some serious money, and by the last race, he knew his wildest dreams were going to come true. He made a quick stop at the ATM and withdrew every penny he owned, and awaited the priest's blessing that would tell him which horse to place the bet on.

True to his pattern, the priest stepped out onto the track before the last race and blessed the forehead, eyes, ears and hooves of one of the horses. George placed his bet — every cent he owned — and watched the horse come in dead last.

George was dumbfounded. He made his way to the track, and when he found the priest, he demanded, "What happened, Father? All day you blessed horses and they won. Then the last race, you bless a horse and he loses. Now I've lost my life savings, thanks to you!!"

The priest nodded wisely and said, "That's the problem with you Protestants… you can't tell the difference between a simple blessing and the Last Rites!"

*   *   *

One Sunday after church, Mom asked her very young daughter what the lesson was about.

Her daughter answered, "Don't be scared, you'll get your quilts."

Needless to say, Mom was perplexed.

Later in the day, the Pastor stopped by for tea.

Mom asked him what that morning's Sunday school lesson was about. He said "Be not afraid, the Comforter is coming."

*   *   *

Three Italian nuns die and go to heaven where they are met at the Pearly Gates by St. Peter. He says, "Ladies, you all led such wonderful lives that I am granting you six months to go back to earth and be anyone you want."

The first nun says, "I want to be Sophia Loren" and *poof* she's gone.

The second nun says, "I want to be Madonna" and *poof* she's gone.

The third nun says, "I want to be Sara Pipalini."

St. Peter looks perplexed. "Who?" he says.

"Sara Pipalini" replies the nun.

St. Peter shakes his head and says, "I'm sorry but that name doesn't ring a bell."

The nun then takes a newspaper out of her habit and hands it to St. Peter.

He reads the paper and starts laughing. He hands it back to her and says, "No, Sister, this says 'Sahara Pipeline' laid by 1,900 men in 6 months!"

*   *   *

Get Me A Priest!
A bus on a busy street in New York City strikes a man. He is lying near death on the sidewalk as a crowd of spectators gathers around.

"Somebody get me a priest!" the man gasps.

A policeman checks the crowd.

"A priest, PLEASE!" the dying man says again.

Then out of the crowd steps a little old Jewish man of at least eighty years of age.

"Mr. Policeman," says the man, "I'm not a priest. I'm not even a Catholic. But for fifty years now I'm living behind St. Elizabeth's Catholic Church on First Avenue, and every night I'm listening to the Catholic litany. Maybe I can be of some comfort to this man."

The policeman agreed and brought the octogenarian over to where the dying man lay.

He kneels down, leans over the injured and says in a solemn voice, "B-4. I-19. N-38. G-54. O-72."

*   *   *

The Pope and President Clinton

Last week a very important meeting took place among God, the Pope, and Moses.

They were troubled because the President of the United States was behaving in an inappropriate manner. They decided that the only course of action was to create an 11th Commandment.

But the problem remained, exactly how to word this new commandment so that it matched the other commandments in style and holy inspiration.

After great meditation and discussion, they finally got it right:

"THOU SHALT NOT COMFORT THY ROD WITH THY STAFF"

*   *   *

A pompous Baptist minister was seated next to an attorney on a flight to Wichita. After the plane was airborne, drink orders were taken. The attorney asked for a whiskey and soda, which was brought and placed before him.

The flight attendant then asked the minister if he would also like a drink. He replied in disgust, "I'd rather be savagely raped by a brazen whore than let liquor touch these lips."

The attorney then handed his drink back to the flight attendant and said, "I didn't know there was a choice."

* * *

Jesus' Dad's Name

A Sunday school teacher asked her class, "What was Jesus' mother's name?"

One child answered, "Mary."

The teacher then asked, "Who knows what Jesus' father's name was?"

A little kid said, "Verge."

Confused, the teacher asked, "Where did you get that?"

The kid said "Well, you know they are always talking about Verge 'n' Mary."

* * *

Two priests died at the same time and met St. Peter at the Pearly Gates.

St. Peter said, "I'd like to get you guys in now, but our computer is down. You'll have to go back to earth for about a week, but you can't go back as priests. What will it be?

The first priest says, "I've always wanted to be an eagle, soaring above the Rocky Mountains."

"So be it," says St. Peter and off flies the first priest.

The second priest mulls this over for a moment, and asks, "Will any of this week 'count', St. Peter?"

"No, I told you the computer is down. There is no way we can keep track of what you're doing."

"In that case," says the second priest, "I've always wanted to be a stud."

"So be it" says St. Peter and the second priest disappears.

A week goes by... the computer is fixed... and the Lord tells St. Peter to recall the two priests. "Will you have any difficulty in locating them?" He asks.

"The first one should be easy," says St. Peter. "He's somewhere over the Rockies flying with the eagles. But the second one, well, that could prove to be more difficult."

"Why?" asketh the Lord.

"He's on a snow tire somewhere in Buffalo, New York."

*   *   *

A little boy was overheard praying: "Lord, if you can't make me a better boy, don't worry about it. I'm having a real good time like I am."

*   *   *

What I Learned in Hebrew School and What I Learned in Catechism

These are written by children and have not been retouched or corrected, poor spelling and all!

1. Solomon, one of David's sons, had 300 wives and 700 porcupines.

2. Jesus was born because Mary had an immaculate contraption.

3. Jesus enunciated the Golden Rule, which says to do one to others before they do one to you.

4. It was a miracle when Jesus rose from the dead and managed to get the tombstone off the entrance.

5. The epistles were the wives of the apostles.

6. St. Peter cavorted to Christianity. He preached holy acrimony, which is another name for marriage.

7. Most religions teach us to have only one spouse. This is called monotony.

8. When Mary heard she was the mother of Jesus, she sang the Magna Carta.

9. When the three wise guys from the east side arrived, they found Jesus in the manager.

10. St. John the blacksmith dumped water on his head.

11. Jesus also explained, a man doth not live by sweat alone.

12. One of the oppossums was St. Matthew who was also a taximan.

*   *   *

People want the front of the bus, the back of the church, and the center of attention.

*   *   *

A father was approached by his small son, who told him proudly, "I know what the Bible means!" His father smiled and replied, "What do you mean, you 'know' what the Bible means?"

The son replied, "I do know!"

"Okay," said his father. "So, son, what does the Bible mean?"

"That's easy, Daddy. It stands for 'Basic Information Before Leaving Earth'."

*   *   *

A man suffered a serious heart attack and had open heart bypass surgery. He awakened from the surgery to find himself in the care of nuns at a Catholic hospital.

As he was recovering, a nun asked him questions regarding how he was going to pay for services. He was asked if he had health insurance. He replied, in a raspy voice, "No health insurance." The nun asked if he had money in the bank. He replied, "No money in the bank." The nun asked "do you have a relative who could help you?" He said, "I only have a spinster sister, who is a nun."

The nun got a little perturbed and announced loudly, "Nuns are not spinsters! Nuns are married to God."

The patient replied, "Send the bill to my brother-in-law."

*   *   *

A little boy was attending his first wedding.

After the service, his cousin asked him, "How many women can a man marry?"

"Sixteen", the boy responded. His cousin was amazed that he had an answer so quickly. "How do you know that?"

"Easy," the little boy said, "All you have to do is add it up, like the Bishop said: 4 better, 4 worse, 4 richer, 4 poorer."

*   *   *

I was shocked, confused, bewildered
As I entered Heaven's door,
Not by the beauty of it all,
By the lights or its décor.

But it was the folks in Heaven
Who made me sputter and gasp —
The thieves, the liars, the sinners,
The alcoholics, the trash.

There stood the kid from seventh grade
Who swiped my lunch money twice.
Next to him was my old neighbor
Who never said anything nice.

Herb, who I always thought
Was rotting away in hell
Was sitting pretty on cloud nine,

Looking incredibly well.

I nudged Jesus, "What's the deal?
I would love to hear Your take.
How'd all these sinners get up here?
God must've made a mistake.

And why's everyone so quiet,
So somber? Give me a clue."
"Hush, child," said He. "They're all in shock.
No one thought they'd see you."

Judge NOT.....

*   *   *

A Sunday School teacher began her lesson with a question,
"Boys and girls, what do we know about God?"
A hand shot up in the air. "He is an artist!" said the kindergarten
boy.
"Really? How do you know?" the teacher asked.
"You know — Our Father, who does art in Heaven...."

*   *   *

FORE!

A golfer in Ireland hit a bad hook into the woods. Looking
for the ball, he discovered a leprechaun flat on his back, a big
bump on his head, and the golfer's ball beside him. Horrified,
the golfer took his water bottle from his belt and poured it
over the little guy, reviving him.

"Arrgh! Wha happen?" the leprechaun says. "Oh, I see. Waal,

ye got me fair and square. Ye get three wishes. Whaddya want?"

"Thank God, you're all right!" the golfer answers in relief. "I don't want anything. I'm glad you're okay, and I apologize. I didn't mean to hit you." And the golfer walks off.

"What a nice guy," the leprechaun says to himself. "But it was fair and square that he got me, and I have to do something for him. I'll give him three things I would want — a great golf game, all the money he ever needs, and a fantastic sex life."

A year goes by (as it does in jokes like this) and the golfer is back, hits another bad ball into the woods and finds the leprechaun waiting for him. "Twas me that made ye hit the ball here," the little guy says. "I wanted to ask ye, how's yer golf game?"

"That's the first bad ball I've hit in a year! I'm a famous international golfer now," the golfer answers. "By the way, it's good to see you're all right."

"Oh, I'm fine now, thankee. I did that fer yer golf game. And tell me how's yer money?"

"Why, I win fortunes in golf. But if I need cash, I just reach in my pocket and pull out $100 bills all day long."

"I did that fer ye. And how's yer sex life?"

The golfer blushes, turns his head away in embarrassment, and says shyly, "Errr, all right, I suppose."

"C'mon, c'mon now. I'm wanting to know if I did a good job. How many times a day?"

Blushing even more, the golfer whispers, "Once… sometimes, twice a week."

"What?!" says the leprechaun in shock. "That's all? Once or twice a week?"

"Well," says the golfer, "I figure that's not too bad for a Catholic priest in a small parish."

*   *   *

Terri asked her Sunday School class to draw pictures of their favorite Bible stories. She was puzzled by Kyle's picture, which showed four people on an airplane, so she asked him which story it was meant to represent.

"I see… and that must be Mary, Joseph, and Baby Jesus, " Ms. Terri said. "But who's the fourth person?"

"Oh, that's Pontius-the-Pilot."

*   *   *

Kathlick?

Three little boys were concerned because they couldn't get anyone to play with them. They decided it was because they had not been baptized and didn't go to Sunday school. So, they went to the nearest church. But only the janitor was there.

One little boy said, "We need to be baptized because no one will come out and play with us. Will you baptize us?"

"Sure," said the janitor

He took them into the bathroom and dunked their little heads in the toilet bowl, one at a time. Then he said, "You are now baptized."

When they got outside, one of them asked, "What religion do you think we are?"

The oldest one said,"We're not Kathlick, because they pour the water on you. We're not Babtis, because they dunk all of you in the water. We're not Methdiss, because they just sprinkle water on you. "

The littlest one said, "Didn't you smell that water?" They all joined in asking, "Yeah, so what do you think that means?"

"I think it means we're Pisscopailians."

*　　　*　　　*

Moshe took his Passover lunch to eat outside in the park. He sat down on a bench and began eating. A little while later a blind man came and sat down next to him. Feeling neighborly, Moshe passed a sheet of matzo to the blind man. The blind man handled the matzo for a few minutes, looked puzzled, and finally exclaimed, "Who wrote this shit?"

*　　　*　　　*

Church Bulletin

Miss Charlene Mason sang 'I Will Not Pass This Way Again', giving obvious pleasure to the congregation.

*   *   *

Presbyterian, Methodist, and Southern Baptist

A Presbyterian, a Methodist, and a Southern Baptist and their wives were all on a cruise together. A tidal wave came up and swamped the ship, and all the couples drowned. The next thing you know, they're standing before St. Peter at the Pearly Gates to be judged.

As fate would have it, the first in line was the Presbyterian and his wife. St. Peter shook his head sadly and said, "I can't let you in. You were moral and upright, but you loved money too much. You loved it so much, you even married a woman named Penny." St. Peter waves sadly, and poof! Down the chute to the 'Other Place' they went.

Then came the Methodist. "Sorry, can't let you in either, " said St. Peter. "You abstained from liquor and dancing and cards, but you loved food too much. You loved food so much you even married a woman named Candy!" Sadly, St. Peter waved again, and whang! Down the chute went the Methodists.

The Southern Baptist turned to his wife and whispered nervously, "It ain't looking good, Fanny."

*   *   *

An elderly man walks into a confessional. The following conversation ensues:
Man: "I am 92 years old, have a wonderful wife of 70 years,

many children, grandchildren, and great-grandchildren. Yesterday, I picked up two college girls, hitchhiking. We went to a motel, where I had sex with each of them three times."

Priest: "Are you sorry for your sins?"

Man: "What sins?"

Priest: "What kind of a Catholic are you?"

Man: "I'm Jewish."

Priest: " Then why are you telling me all this?"

Man: "I'm telling everybody!"

*   *   *

Church Bulletin

Thursday at 5:00 p.m. there will be a meeting of the Little Mothers Club. All wishing to become Little Mothers, please see the minister in his study.

*   *   *

Wee Ones

Mrs. Donovan was walking down O'Connell Street in Dublin when she met up with Father Flaherty.

The Father said, "Top o' the mornin' to ye! Aren't ye Mrs. Donovan and didn't I marry ye and yer husband two years ago?"

She replied, "Aye, that ye did, Father."

The Father asked, "And be there any wee ones yet?"

She replied, "No, not yet, Father."

The Father said, "Well now, I'm going to Rome next week and I'll light a candle for ye and yer husband."

She replied, "Oh, thank ye, Father."

They parted ways. Some years later they met again. The Father asked, "Well now, Mrs. Donovan, how are ye these days?"

She replied, "Oh, very well, Father!"

The Father asked, "And tell me, have ye any wee ones yet?"

She replied, "Oh yes, Father! Three sets of twins and four singles, 10 in all!"

The Father said, "That's wonderful! How is yer loving husband doing?"

She replied, "'E's gone to Rome to blow out yer fookin' candle."

*   *   *

Church Bulletin

At the evening service tonight, the sermon topic will be "What is Hell?" Come early and listen to our choir practice.

*   *   *

Holy Water

One morning a man comes into the church on crutches, stops in front of the holy water and splashes some of it on both of his legs and then throws away his crutches. An altar boy witnessed the scene and runs to the rectory to tell the priest what he's just seen. Without batting an eye, the priest says, "Son, you've witnessed a miracle. Tell me, where is this man?"

"Flat on his ass, Father, over by the holy water."

*   *   *

Tuna and Rye Bread

Mother Teresa died and went to Heaven. God greeted her at the Pearly Gates. "Art thou hungry, Mother Teresa?" asks God.

"I could eat," Mother Teresa replies.

So God opens a can of tuna and reaches for a chunk of rye bread and they share it. While eating this humble meal, Mother Teresa looks down into Hell and sees the inhabitants devouring huge steaks, lobsters, pheasants, pastries and wines. Curious, but deeply trusting, she remains quiet.

The next day God again invites her to join him for a meal. Again, it is tuna and rye bread. Once again, Mother Teresa can see the denizens of Hell enjoying caviar, champagne, lamb, truffles, and chocolates. Still she says nothing.

The following day, mealtime arrives and another can of tuna is opened. She can't contain herself any longer. Meekly, she says: "God, I am grateful to be in Heaven with You as a reward for the pious, obedient life I led. But here in Heaven all I get to eat is tuna and a piece of rye bread and in the Other Place they eat like emperors and kings! I just don't understand."

God sighs. "Let's be honest," He says, "for just two people, does it pay to cook?"

*   *   *

Sister Mary, who worked for a home health agency, was out making her rounds visiting homebound patients when she ran out of gas. As luck would have it, a gas station was just a block away. She walked to the station to borrow a gas can and bought some gas.

The attendant told her the only gas can he owned had been loaned out but she could wait until it was returned. Since the nun was on the way to see a patient, she decided not to wait and walked back to her car. She looked for something in her car that she could fill with gas and spotted the bedpan she was taking to the patient.

Always resourceful, she carried the bedpan to the station, filled it with gas and carried the full bedpan back to her car. As she was pouring the gas into her tank, two men watched from across the street.

One of them turned to the other and said, "If that starts, I'm turning Catholic."

*   *   *

And elderly woman died last month. Having never married, she requested no male pallbearers. In her handwritten instructions for her memorial service, she wrote, "They wouldn't take me out while I was alive, I don't want them to take me out when I'm dead."

*   *   *

The Origin of Pets

A newly discovered chapter in the Book of Genesis has provided the answer to "Where do pets come from?"

Adam and Eve said, "Lord, when we were in the garden, you walked with us every day. Now we do not see you anymore. We are lonesome here, and it is difficult for us to remember how much you love us."

and God said, "No problem! I willcreate a companion for you that will be with you forever and who will be a reflection of my love for you, so that you will love me even when you cannot see me. Regardless of how selfish or childish or unlovable you may be, this new companion will accept you as you are and will love you as I do, in spite of yourselves."

And God created a new animal to be a companion for Adam and Eve. And it was a good animal. And God was pleased. And the new animal was pleased to be with Adam and Eve and he wagged his tail.

And Adam said, "Lord, I have already named all the animals in the Kingdom and I cannot think of a name for this new animal." And God said, "No problem. Because I have created this new animal to be a reflection of my love for you, his name will be a reflection of my own name and, you will call him DOG."

And Dog lived with Adam and Eve and was a companion to them and loved them. And they were comforted. And God was pleased. And Dog was content and wagged its tail.

After a while, it came to pass that an angel came to the Lord and said, "Lord, Adam and Eve have become filled with pride. They strut and preen like peacocks and they believe they are worthy of adoration. Dog has indeed taught them that they are loved, but perhaps too well."

And God said, "No problem! I will create for them a companion who will be with them forever and who will see them as they are. The companion will remind them of their limitations, so they will know that they are not always worthy of adoration."

And God created CAT to be a companion to Adam and Eve. And Cat would not obey them. And when Adam and Eve gazed into Cat's eyes, they were reminded that they were not the supreme beings. And Adam and Eve learned humility. And they were greatly improved. And God was pleased. And Dog was happy. And Cat didn't give a shit one way or the other.

*   *   *

Two boys were walking home from Sunday school after hearing a strong preaching on the devil. One said to the other, "What do you think about all this Satan stuff?"

The other boy replied, "Well, you know how Santa Claus turned out. It's probably just your dad."

*   *   *

Monastery Life

A young monk arrives at the monastery. He is assigned to helping the other monks in copying the old canons and laws of the church by hand.

He notices, however, that all of the monks are copying from copies, not from the original manuscript. So, the new monk goes to the head abbot to question this, pointing out that if someone made even a small error in the first copy, it would never be picked up. In fact, that error would be continued in all of the subsequent copies.

The head monk says, "We have been copying from the copies for centuries, but you make a good point, my son."

He goes down into the dark caves underneath the monastery where the original manuscripts are held as archives in a locked vault that hasn't been opened for hundreds of years. Hours go by and nobody sees the old abbot.

So, the young monk gets worried and goes down to look for him. He sees him banging his head against the wall and wailing, "We missed the R! We missed the R! We missed the R!" His forehead is all bloody and bruised and he is crying uncontrollably.

The young monks asks the old abbot, "What's wrong, Father?"

With a choking voice, the old abbot replies, "The word was....

CELEBRATE!!!"

*　　　　*　　　　*

It was Palm Sunday and because of a sore throat, five-year-old Johnny stayed home from church with a sitter. When the family returned home, they were carrying several palm branches. The boy asked what they were for.

"People held them over Jesus' head as he walked by."

"Wouldn't you know it," the boy fumed, "the one Sunday I don't go, He shows up!"

*　　　　*　　　　*

The Bible Salesmen

A minister concluded that his church was getting into serious financial troubles. Coincidentally, by chance, while checking the church storeroom, he discovered several cartons of new bibles that had never been opened and distributed. So at his Sunday sermon, he asked for three volunteers from the congregation who would be willing to sell the bibles door-to-door for $10 each to raise the desperately needed money for the church.

Peter, Paul and Louie all raised their hands to volunteer for the task.

The minister knew that Peter and Paul earned their living as salesmen and were likely capable of selling some bibles, but he had serious doubts about Louie.

Louie was just a little local farmer, who had always tended

to keep to himself because he was embarrassed by his speech impediment. Poor Louie stuttered very badly. But, not wanting to discourage poor Louie, the minister decided to let him try anyway.

He sent the three of them away with the back seat of their cars stacked with bibles and asked them to meet with him and report the results of their door-to-door selling efforts the following Sunday.

Anxious to find out how successful they were, the minister immediately asked Peter, "Well, Peter, how did you make out selling our bibles last week?"

Proudly handing the reverend an envelope, Peter replied, "Using my sales prowess, I was able to sell 20 bibles and here's the $200 I collected on behalf of the church."

"Fine job, Peter!" the minister said, vigorously shaking his hand. "You are indeed a fine salesman and the church is indebted to you."

Turning to Paul, he asked, "And, Paul, how many bibles did you manage to sell for the church last week?"

Paul, smiling and sticking out his chest, confidently replied, "I am a professional salesman and was happy to give the church the benefit of my sales expertise. Last week I sold 28 bibles on behalf of the church, and here's the $280 I collected."

The minister responded, "That's absolutely splendid, Paul.

You are truly a professional salesman and the church is also indebted to you."

Apprehensively, the minister turned to Louie and said, "And Louie, did you manage to sell any bibles last week?"

Louie silently offered the minister a large envelope. The reverend opened it and counted the contents. "What is this?" the minister exclaimed, "Louie, there's $3200 in here! Are you suggesting that you sold 320 bibles for the church, door-to-door, in just one week?"

Louie nodded.

"That's impossible!" both Peter and Paul said in unison. "We are professional salesmen, yet you claim to have sold 20 times as many bibles as we could."

"Yes, this does seem unlikely, " the minister agreed. "I think you'd better explain how you managed to accomplish this, Louie."

Louie shrugged. "I-I-I re-re-really do-do-don't kn-kn-know f-f-f-for sh-sh-sh-sure, " he stammered.

Impatiently, Peter interrupted. "For crying out loud, Louie, just tell us what you said to them when they answered the door!"

"A-a-a-all I-I-I s-s-said wa-wa-was," Louie replied, "W-w-would y-y-you l-l-l-like t-t-to b-b-buy th-th-this b-b-b-b-bible f-f-for t-t-ten b-b-b-bucks ——- o-o-or wo-wo-would yo-you j-j-just l-l-like m-m-me t-t-to st-st-stand h-h-here and r-r-r-read it t-t-to y-y-you?"

*　　　*　　　*

First Time Ushers

A little boy in church for the first time watched as the ushers passed around the offering plates.

When they came near his pew, the boy said loudly, "Don't pay for me, Daddy. I'm under five."

*　　　*　　　*

Why Catholic Schools Should Teach Sex-Ed

Mother Superior called all the nuns together one evening and said to them: "I must tell you all something. We have a case of gonorrhea in the convent."

"Thank God," said an elderly nun at the back. "I'm so sick of Chardonnay."

*　　　*　　　*

Two prostitutes were riding around town with a sign on top of their car that said, "Two prostitutes - $50.00."

A policeman, seeing the sign, stopped them and told them they'd either have to remove the sign or go to jail.

Just at that time, another car passed with a sign saying, "Jesus saves."

One of the girls asked the cop, "How come you don't stop them?!"

"Well, that's a little different," the cop smiled. "Their sign pertains to religion."

So the two ladies of the night frowned as they took their sign down and drove off.

The following day found the same cop in the area when he noticed the two ladies driving around with a large sign on their car again.

Figuring he had an easy bust, he began to catch up with them when he noticed the new sign, which read: "Two angels seeking Peter - $50.00"

*　　　*　　　*

Brothel Trip

Bill Lassegard goes into a brothel and tells the madam he would like a young girl for the night. Surprised, she looks at him and asks, "How old are you?"

"I'm 80 years old," he says.

"80!" replies the woman, "Don't you realize you've had it?"

"Oh, sorry," says Bill, "How much do I owe you?"

*　　　*　　　*

Children's Sermon

One Easter Sunday morning as the minister was preaching the children's sermon, he reached into his bag of props and pulled out an egg. He pointed at the egg and asked the children, "What's in here?"

"I know!" a little boy exclaimed, "Pantyhose!"

*   *   *

A Sunday school teacher was discussing the Ten Commandments with her five and six year olds. After explaining the commandment to honor thy father and thy mother, she asked, "Is there a commandment that teaches us how to treat our brothers and sisters?"

Without missing a beat, one little boy answered, "Thou shalt not kill."

*   *   *

A limo driver, after getting all of Pope Benedict's luggage loaded into the limo (and he doesn't travel light) notices that the Pope is still standing on the curb. "Excuse me, Your Eminence," says the driver, "Would you please take your seat so we can leave?"

"Well, to tell you the truth," says the Pope, "they never let me drive at the Vatican, and I'd really like to drive today."

"I'm sorry but I cannot let you do that; I'd lose my job! What if something should happen?" protests the driver, wishing he'd never gone to work that morning.

"There might be something extra in it for you," says the Pope.

Reluctantly, the driver gets in the back as the Pope climbs in behind the wheel.

The driver quickly regrets his decision when, after exiting the airport, the Supreme Pontiff floors it, accelerating the limo to 105 mph.

"Please slow down, Your Holiness!!" pleads the worried driver, but the Pope keeps the pedal to the metal until they hear sirens.

"Oh my God, I'm gonna lose my license," moans the driver.

The Pope pulls over and rolls down the window as the cop approaches, but the cop takes one look at him, goes back to his motorcycle and gets on the radio.

"I need to talk to the Chief," he says to the dispatcher. The Chief gets on the radio and the cop tells him that he's stopped a limo going a hundred and five. "So bust him," said the Chief. "I don't think we want to do that, he's really important," said the cop. The Chief then asked, "Who ya got there, the Mayor?"
Cop: "Bigger"
Chief: "Governor?"
Cop: "Bigger"
Chief: "Senator?"
Cop: "Bigger"
"Well," said the Chief, "who is it?"
Cop: "I think it's Jesus!"
Chief: "What makes you think it's Jesus?"
Cop: "He's got the Pope for a limo driver!"

*   *   *

There were five country churches in a small Texas town:

the Presbyterian Church, the Baptist Church, the Methodist Church, the Catholic Church, and the Jewish Synagogue. Each church was overrun with pesky squirrels.

One day, the Presbyterian Church called a meeting to decide what to do about the squirrels. After much prayer and consideration they determined that the squirrels were predestined to be there and they shouldn't interfere with God's divine will.

In the Baptist Church, the squirrels had taken up habitation in the baptistery. The deacons met and decided to put a cover on the baptistery and drown the squirrels in it. The squirrels escaped somehow and there were twice as many there the next week.

The Methodist Church got together and decided that they were not in a position to harm any of God's creation. So, they humanely trapped the squirrels and set them free a few miles outside of town. Three days later, the squirrels were back.

But the Catholic Church came up with the best and most effective solution.

They baptized the squirrels and registered them as members of the church. Now they only see them on Christmas and Easter.

Not much was heard about the Jewish Synagogue, but they took one squirrel and had a short service with him called circumcision.

*　　*　　*

A minister was completing a temperance sermon. With great emphasis he said, "If I had all the beer in the world, I'd take it and pour it into the river." With even greater emphasis he said, "And if I had all the wine in the world, I'd take it and pour it into the river." And then finally shaking his fist in the air, he said, "And if I had all the whiskey in the world, I'd take it and pour it into the river."

Sermon complete, he sat down. The song leader stood very cautiously and announced with a smile, nearly laughing, "For our closing song, let us sing hymn # 365, We Shall Gather at the River."

*   *   *

Church Bulletin

Next Thursday there will be tryouts for the choir. They need all the help they can get.

*   *   *

Today's Blessing

May the fleas of a thousand camels infest the crotch of the person who screws up your day and may their arms be too short to scratch.
Amen

*   *   *

The man wearing a fabulous vintage chiffon-lined Dior gold lamé gown, over a silk Vera Wang empire-waist tulle cocktail dress, accessorized with a three-foot, beaded, peaked House of Whoville hat, along with the ruby slippers that Judy Garland wore in *The Wizard of Oz* is worried that *The DaVinci Code* might make the Roman Catholic Church look foolish.

* * *

A man went to church one day and afterward he stopped to shake the preacher's hand. He said, "Preacher, I'll tell you, that was a damned fine sermon. Damned good!"

The preacher said, "Thank you sir, but I'd rather you didn't use that kind of language in the Lord's house."

The man said, "I was so damned impressed with that sermon that I put five thousand dollars in the offering plate!"

The preacher said, "No shit?"

* * *

Did you know that it's wrong for a woman to make coffee? Yup, it's in the Bible. It says...... "Hebrews!"

* * *

Announcement in a church bulletin for a national Prayer and Fasting Conference: "The cost for attending the Fasting and Prayer conference includes meals."

* * *

Blind Man

Two nuns are ordered to paint a room in the convent, and the last instruction of the Mother Superior is that they must not get even a drop of paint on their habits.

After conferring about this for a while, the two nuns decide to lock the door of the room, strip off their habits, and paint in the nude.

In the middle of the project, there comes a knock at the door. "Who is it?" calls one of the nuns.

"Blind man," replies a voice from the other side of the door.

The two nuns look at each other and shrug and, deciding that no harm can come from letting a blind man into the room, they open the door.

"Nice boobs," says the man. "Where do you want the blinds?"

*   *   *

Church Lady

The church was full. A young woman with a wonderful figure, and not nearly enough clothes to hide it all, came in late. She strode down the center aisle, close to the front, and sat down. It was plain to the preacher that he had lost all the men at this service to this voluptuous beauty. He shook a fist at her and said, "You are the Jezebel the Good Book tells us about. You have captured the mind of every man in this building with evil thought. But, I am a man of God! You don't affect me, and right now up in Heaven, you brazen woman, Saint Finger is shaking his Peter at you!"

*   *   *

A nun was going to Chicago. She went to the airport and sat down waiting for her flight. She looked over in the corner and saw one of those weight machines that tells your fortune.

So, she thought to herself, "I'll give it a try just to see what it tells me." She went over to the machine and put her nickel in, and out came a card that said, "You're a nun, you weigh 128 lbs., and you are going to Chicago."

She sat back down and thought about it. She told herself it probably tells everyone the same thing, but decided to try it again. She went back to the machine and put her nickel in. Out came a card reading, "You're a nun, you weigh 128 lbs., you're going to Chicago, and you are going to play a fiddle."

The nun said to herself, "I know that's wrong. I have never played a musical instrument a day in my life." She sat back down and from nowhere a cowboy came over and sat his fiddle case down next to her. The nun picked up the fiddle and started playing beautiful music. Startled, she looked back at the machine and said, "This is incredible. I've got to try it again."

Back to the machine, she put her nickel in and another card came out. It said, "You're a nun, you weigh 128 lbs., you're going to Chicago, and you're going to break wind." Now, the nun knows the machine is wrong. "I never broke wind in public a day in my life!" Well, she tripped, fell off the scales and broke wind.

Stunned, she sat back down and looked at the machine. She said to herself, "This is truly unbelievable! I've got to try it again." She went back to the machine, put her nickel in and collected the card. It said, "You're a nun, you weigh 128 lbs., you have fiddled and farted around and missed your flight to Chicago!!"

*   *   *

Attending a wedding for the first time, a little girl whispered to her mother, "Why is the bride dressed in white?"

Because white is the color of happiness, and today is the happiest day of her life."

The child thought about this for a moment, then said, "So why is the groom wearing black?"

*   *   *

On the outskirts of a small town, there was a big old pecan tree just inside the cemetery fence. One day, two boys filled up a bucketful of nuts and sat down by the tree, out of sight, and began dividing the nuts.

"One for you, one for me. One for you, one for me, " said one boy.

Several dropped and rolled down toward the fence. Another boy came riding along the road on his bicycle. As he passed, he thought he heard voices from inside the cemetery. He slowed down to investigate. Sure enough, he heard, "one for you, one for me. One for you, one for me."

He just knew what it was. "Oh my," he shuddered, "it's Satan and the Lord dividing the souls at the cemetery." He jumped back on his bike and rode off. Just around the bend he met an old man with a cane, hobbling along. "Come here quick, " said the boy. "You won't believe what I heard! Satan and the Lord are down at the cemetery dividing up the souls." The man said, "Beat it kid, can't you see it's hard for me to walk." When the boy insisted though, the man hobbled to the cemetery. Standing by the fence they heard, "One for you, one for me. One for you, one for me."

The old man whispered, "Boy, you've been telling the truth. Let's see if we can see the Lord himself." Shaking with fear, they peered through the fence, yet were still unable to see anything. The old man and the boy gripped the wrought iron bars of the fence tighter and tighter as they tried to get a glimpse of the Lord.

At last they heard, "One for you, one for me." And one last "One for you, one for me. That's all. Now let's go get those nuts by the fence, and we'll be done."

They say the old man made it back to town a full two minutes ahead of the boy on the bike!

*   *   *

One Sunday a pastor asked his congregation to consider giving a little extra in the offering plate. He said that whoever gave the most would be able to pick out three hymns. He noticed that someone had contributed a $1000 bill. He was so excited that he immediately shared his joy with his congregation and said he'd like to personally thank the person who had placed the money in the plate.

A very quiet elderly, saintly widow shyly raised her hand. The pastor asked her to come to the front. Slowly she made her way to the pastor. He told her how wonderful it was that she gave so much and asked her to pick out three hymns.

Her eyes brightened as she looked over the congregation,

pointed to the three handsomest men in the building and said, "I'll take him and him and him."

*   *   *

A little girl became restless as the preacher's sermon dragged on and on. Finally she leaned over to her mother and whispered, "Mommy, if we give him the money now, will he let us go?"

*   *   *

While walking down the street one day a senator is tragically hit by a truck and dies. His soul arrives in heaven and is met by St. Peter at the entrance. "Welcome to Heaven, " says St. Peter. "Before you settle in, it seems there is a problem. We seldom see a high official around these parts, you see, so we're not sure what to do with you."

"No problem, just let me in," says the now former senator.

"Well, I'd like to but I have orders from higher up. What we'll do is have you spend one day in Hell and one day in Heaven. Then you can choose where to spend eternity."

"Really, I've made up my mind. I want to be in Heaven," says the senator.

"I'm sorry, but we have our rules." And with that, St. Peter escorts him to the elevator and he goes down, down, down to Hell. The doors open, and he finds himself in the middle of a green golf course. In the distance is the clubhouse and standing in front of it are all his friends and other politicians who had worked with him; everyone is very happy and in evening dress. They run to greet him, hug him and reminisce about the good times they had while getting rich at the expense of the people. They play a friendly game of golf and then dine on lobster and caviar. Also present is the Devil, who really is a very friendly guy who had a good time dancing and telling jokes. They are having such a good time that before realizes it, it is time to go. Everyone gives him a big hug and waves while the elevator rises. The elevator goes up, up, up and the door re-opens on Heaven where St. Peter is waiting for him. "Now, it's time to visit Heaven."

So 24 hours pass with the senator joining a group of contented souls moving from cloud to cloud, playing the harp and singing. They have a good time and before he realizes it, the hours have gone by and St. Peter returns. "Well, then, you've spent a day in Hell and a day in Heaven. Have you decided?"

The politician reflects for a minute, then answers: "Well, I would never have said it, I mean, Heaven has been delightful, but I think I would be better off in Hell."

So, St. Peter escorts him to the elevator and he goes down, down, down to Hell. Now the doors of the elevator open and he is in the middle of a barren land covered with waste and garbage. He sees all of his friends, dressed in rags, picking up the trash and putting it in black bags. The Devil comes over to him and lays his arm on his neck.

"I don't understand," stammers the senator. "Yesterday I was here and there was a golf course and clubhouse and we ate lobster and caviar and danced and had a great time. Now there is a wasteland full of garbage and my friends look miserable."

The Devil looks at him, smiles and says, "Yesterday we were campaigning. Today you voted for us!"

*   *   *

My guardian angel helps me with math, but he's not much good for science.
- Henry, age 8

*   *   *

Dog Prayers

Dear God,
We dogs can understand human verbal instructions, hand signals, whistles, horns, clickers, beepers, scent ID's, electromagnetic energy field and Frisbee flight patterns. What do humans understand?

Dear God,
More meatballs, less spaghetti, please.

Dear God,
Are there mailmen in Heaven? If there are, will I have to apologize?

Dear God,
Let me give you a list of just some of the things I must remember to be a good dog:

1. I will not eat the cat's food before they eat it or after they throw it up.
2. I will not roll on dead seagulls, fish, crabs, etc., just because I like the way they smell.

3. I will not munch on "leftovers" in the kitty litter box, although they are tasty.

4. The diaper pail is not a cookie jar.

5. The sofa is not a face towel, neither are Mom and Dad's laps.

6. I will not bite the officer's hand when he reaches in for Mom's driver's license and registration.

7. I will not play tug-of-war with Dad's underwear when he's on the toilet.

8. Sticking my nose into someone's crotch is an unacceptable way of saying "hello".

9. I don't need to suddenly stand straight up when I'm under the coffee table.

10. I must shake the rainwater out of my fur before entering the house, not after.

11. I will not throw up in the car.

12. I will not come in from outside and immediately drag my butt.

13. I will not sit in the middle of the living room and lick my crotch when we have company.

14. The cat is not a 'squeaky toy'. So when I play with him and he makes that noise, it's usually not a good thing.

15. And yes, I do lick them because I can.

And, finally, my last question is:

Dear God,
When I get to Heaven, may I have my testicles back?

*   *   *

While driving in Pennsylvania, a family caught up to an Amish carriage. The owner of the carriage obviously had a sense of humor because attached to the back of the carriage was a hand printed sign:

Energy efficient vehicle: Runs on oats and grass.
Caution: Do not step in exhaust

*   *   *

I only know the names of two angels: Hark and Harold
- Gregory, age 5

*   *   *

A college drama group presented a play in which one character would stand on a trapdoor and announce, "I descend into hell!" A stagehand below would then pull a rope, the trapdoor would open, and the character would plunge through. The play was well received.

When the actor playing the part became ill, another actor who was quite overweight took his place. When the new actor announced, "I descend into hell!" the stagehand pulled the rope, and the actor began his plunge, but became hopelessly stuck. No amount of tugging on the rope could make him descend. One student in the balcony jumped up and yelled: "Hallelujah! Hell is full!"

*   *   *

Bubba Knows Everybody
Bubba was bragging to his boss one day, "You know, I know everyone there is to know. Just name someone, anyone and I know them."

Tired of his boasting, his boss called his bluff, "OK, Bubba, how about Tom Cruise?" "Sure, yes, Tom and I are old friends, and I can prove it." So Bubba and his boss fly out to Hollywood and knock on Tom Cruise's door, and sure enough, Tom Cruise, shouts, "Bubba! Great to see you! You and your friend come right in and join me for lunch!" Although impressed, Bubba's boss is still skeptical. After they leave Cruise's house, he tells Bubba that he thinks Bubba's knowing Cruise was just lucky.

"No, no, just name anyone else," Bubba says. "President Clinton," his boss quickly retorts. "Yes," Bubba says, "I know him, let's fly out to Washington." And off they go. At the White House, Clinton spots Bubba on the tour and motions him and his boss over, saying, "Bubba, what a surprise; I was just on my way to a meeting, but you and your friend come on in and let's have a cup of coffee first and catch up." Well, the boss is very shaken by now, but still not totally convinced. After they leave the White House grounds, he expresses his doubts to Bubba, who again implores him to name anyone else.

"The Pope," his boss replies. "Sure!" says Bubba. "My folks are from Germany, and I've known the Pope a long time." So off they fly to Rome, Bubba and his boss are assembled with the masses in Vatican Square when Bubba says, "This will never work. I can't catch the Pope's eye among all these people. Tell you what, I know all the guards so let me just go upstairs and I'll come out on the balcony with the Pope." And he disappears into the crowd headed toward the Vatican. Sure enough, half an hour later, Bubba emerges with the

Pope on the balcony. But by the time Bubba returns, he finds that his boss has had a heart attack and is surrounded by paramedics.

Working his way to his boss' side, Bubba asks him, "What happened?" His boss looks up and says, "I was doing fine until you and Pope came out on the balcony and the man next to me said, "Who's that on the balcony with Bubba?"

*   *   *

A father was at the beach with the children when the four-year-old son ran up to him, grabbed his hand, and led him to the shore where a seagull lay dead in the sand. "Daddy, what happened to him?" the son asked.

"He died and went to Heaven," the Dad replied. The boy thought a moment, and then said, "Did God throw him back down?"

*   *   *

Transportation in Heaven

Three men die and go to heaven. At the gate St. Peter tells them, "Before you go into heaven, we are going to give you each a vehicle with which to get around. The way we determine what type of vehicle you will get is by how faithful you were to your wives. Now, "he says, turning to the first man, "were you true to your wife?"

"Yes, I was, St. Peter," says the first man. "I never strayed. From the day I married her to the day I died, I slept with no woman other than my wife. I loved her very deeply."

"As a reward for your complete fidelity, "says St. Peter, "I now give you these keys to a beautiful Rolls Royce."

The man happily accepts the keys, and St. Peter turns to the second man. "Sir, " he says, "were you faithful to your wife?"

"Well, St. Peter, "says the second man a little shyly, "I must admit that when I was much younger, I did stray once or twice. But I did love my wife very much, and after those minor indiscretions, I was completely faithful until my dying day."

St. Peter looks down at the man and says, "As a reward for good marital conduct, I am giving you these keys to a Pontiac."

As the man takes the keys from him, St. Peter turns to the third man, "Sir, " he says, "were you faithful to your wife?"

"St. Peter," says the man, "I screwed everything I could, every chance I got. There wasn't a week of my marriage that I didn't sleep with someone other than my wife. But I must admit to you, St. Peter, that it was a problem I had because I really did love my wife very much."

"Well, " says St. Peter, "we do know that you did love your wife and that does count for something, so this is what you get." With that he rolls out a ten-speed bicycle and gives it to the man. The gates of heaven open, and the three men enter.

Sometime later the man on the bicycle is riding along, when he sees that the man with the Rolls Royce has pulled over and is sitting on the bumper of his car. He is sobbing uncontrollably. The man pulls his bicycle up next to the man and says, "Hey, pal, what's the matter? What could possibly be wrong? You have a beautiful Rolls Royce to drive around in!"

"I know, "says the man through his sobs, "but I just saw my wife on roller skates!"

*   *   *

Father O'Malley answers the phone: "Hello."
"Is this Father O'Malley?"
"It is."
"This is the IRS. Can you help us?"
"I can."
"Do you know a Ted Houlihan?"
"I do."
"Is he a member of your congregation?"
"He is."
"Did he donate $10,000 to the church?"
"He will."

*   *   *

The Nativity in Washington, DC
The Supreme Court has ruled that there cannot be a nativity scene in Washington, D.C. this Christmas. This wasn't for any religious reasons. They simply have not been able to find three wise men and a virgin.

*   *   *

Father Murphy

Father Murphy was playing golf with a parishioner. On the first hole, he sliced into the rough. His opponent heard him mutter "Hoover!" under his breath. On the second hole, the ball went straight into a water hazard. "Hoover!" again, a little louder this time. On the third hole, a miracle occurred, and Fr. Murphy's drive landed on the green only six inches from the hole! "Praise be to God!" He carefully lined up the putt, but the ball curved around the hole instead of going in. "HOOVER!!!!" By this time, his opponent couldn't withhold his curiosity any longer, and asked why the priest said "Hoover". "It's the biggest dam I know!"

*   *   *

It was getting a little crowded in heaven, so God decided to change the admittance policy. The new law was that in order to get into heaven, you had to have a real bummer of a day when you died. The policy would go into effect at noon the next day.

The next day at 12:01, the first person comes to the gates of heaven. The angel at the gate, remembering the new policy, promptly says to the man, "Before I let you in, I need you to tell me how your day was going when you died."

"No problem, " says the man. "I came home to my 25th floor apartment on my lunch hour and caught my wife half-naked and appearing to be having an affair, but her lover was nowhere in sight. I immediately began searching for him. My wife was yelling at me as I searched the entire apartment. Just as I was about to give up, I happened to glance out onto the balcony and noticed that there was a man hanging off the edge by his fingertips! The nerve of that guy! Well, I ran out onto the balcony and stomped on his fingers until he fell to the ground. But wouldn't you know it, he landed in some trees and bushes that broke his fall and he didn't die. This ticked me off even more. In a rage, I went back inside to get the first thing I could get my hands on to throw at him. Oddly enough, the first thing I thought of was the refrigerator. I unplugged it, pushed it out onto the balcony, and tipped it over the side. It plummeted 25 stories and crushed him! The excitement of the moment was so great that I had a heart attack and died almost instantly."

The angel sits back and thinks for a moment. Technically, the guy did have a bad day. It was a crime of passion, so the angel announces, "OK sir. Welcome to the Kingdom of Heaven," and lets him in.

A few seconds later, the next guy comes up. "Before I can let you in, I need to hear about what your day was like when you died."

The man says, "No problem. But you're not going to believe this. I was on the balcony of my 26th floor apartment doing my daily exercises. I had been under a lot of pressure so I was really pushing hard to relieve my stress. I guess I got a little carried away, slipped and accidentally fell over the side! Luckily, I was able to catch myself by the fingertips on the balcony below mine. But all of a sudden this crazy man comes running out of his apartment, starts cussing, and stomps on my fingers. Well, of course, I fell. I hit some trees and bushes at the bottom that broke my fall so I didn't die right away. As I'm lying there face up on the ground, unable to move and in excruciating pain, I see this guy push his refrigerator of all things off the balcony. It falls the 25 floors and lands on top of me, killing me instantly."

The angel is quietly laughing to himself as the man finishes his story. "I could get used to his new policy," he thinks to himself. "Very well, " the angel announces, welcome to the Kingdom of Heaven" and lets the man enter.

A few seconds later, a third man comes up to the gate. The angel is warming up to his task. "OK, please tell me what it was like the day you died."

The man says, "OK, picture this: I'm naked inside this refrigerator."

*   *   *

An eighty-five-year-old couple, married for almost sixty years, died in a car crash. They had been in good health the last ten years, mainly as a result of her interest in health food and exercise. When they reached the Pearly Gates, St. Peter took them to their mansion, which was decked out with a beautiful kitchen and a master bath suite with a sauna and Jacuzzi. As they oohed and aahed, the man asked St. Peter how much all this was going to cost.

"It's free," St. Peter replied. "This is heaven."

Next they went out back to survey the championship golf course that the home backed up to. They would have golfing privileges every day and each week the course would change to a new one that represented one of the great golf courses on earth. The old man asked, "What are the greens fees?"

St. Peter replies, "This is heaven; you play for free."

Next they went to the clubhouse and saw the lavish buffet lunch with the cuisines of the world laid out. "How much to eat?" asked the old man.

"Don't you understand yet? This is heaven; it is free!" St. Peter replied with some exasperation.

"Well, where are the low-fat and low-cholesterol tables?" the old man asked timidly.

St. Peter lectured, "That's the best part; you can eat as much as you like of whatever you like and you never get fat and you never get sick. This is heaven."

With that, the old man threw down his hat, stomped on it, and shrieked wildly. St. Peter and the gent's wife both tried to calm him down, asking him what was wrong. The old man looked at his wife and said, "This is all your fault. If it weren't for your bran muffins, I could have been here ten years ago!"

*   *   *

A man, his wife, and his mother-in-law went on vacation to the Holy Land. While they were there, the mother-in-law passed away.

The undertaker told them, "You can have her shipped home for $5000 or you can bury her here in the Holy Land for $150."

The man thought about it and told him he would just have her shipped home.

The undertaker asked, "Why would you spend $5000 to ship your mother-in-law home, when it would be wonderful to have her buried here and spend only $150?"

The man replied, "A man died here 2000 years ago, was buried here, and three days later he rose from the dead. I just can't take that chance."

*   *   *

A minister waited in line to have his car filled with gas just before a long holiday weekend. The attendant worked quickly, but there were many cars ahead of him. Finally the attendant motioned him toward a vacant pump. "Reverend," said the young man, "I'm so sorry about the delay. It seems as if everyone waits until the last minute to get ready for a long trip."

The minister chuckled, "I know what you mean. It's the same in my business."

*   *   *

Bless This Car

A priest and a rabbi operated a church and a synagogue across the street from each other. Since their schedules intertwined, they decided to go in together to buy a car.

After the purchase, they drove it home and parked it on the street between them.

A few minutes later, the rabbi looked out and saw the priest sprinkling water on their new car. It didn't need a wash, so he hurried out and asked the priest what he was doing. "I'm blessing," the priest replied.

The rabbi considered this a moment, then went back inside the synagogue. He reappeared a moment later with a hacksaw, walked over to the back of the car and cut two inches off the tailpipe!

*   *   *

Amen: the only part of a prayer that everyone knows
Bulletin: Your receipt for attending Mass
Choir: a group of people whose singing allows the rest of the congregation to lip-sync
Holy Water: a liquid whose chemical formula is H2oly
Hymn: a song of praise usually sung in a key three octaves higher than that of the congregation's range
Incense: holy smoke!
Recessional Hymn: the last song at Mass often sung a little more quietly, since most of the people have already left

*   *   *

There were two Catholic boys, Michael Murphy and Antonio Secola, whose lives paralleled each other in amazing ways. In the same year Michael was born in Ireland, Antonio was born in Italy. Faithfully they attended parochial school from kindergarten through their senior year in high school.

They took their vows to enter the priesthood early in college and upon graduation, they both became priests.

Their careers had come to amaze the world, but it was

generally acknowledged that Antonio Secola was just a cut above Michael Murphy in all respects. Their rise through the ranks of bishop, archbishop and finally cardinal was swift to say the least, and the Catholic world knew that when the present Pope died, it would be one of the two who would become the next Pope.

In time the Pope did die and the College of Cardinals went to work. In less time than anyone had expected, white smoke rose from the chimney and the world waited to see whom they had chosen.

The world, Catholic, Protestant and secular, was surprised to learn that Michael Murphy had been elected Pope!

Antonio Secola was beyond surprise. He was devastated because even with all of Michael's gifts, Antonio knew he was the better qualified. With gall that shocked the Cardinals, Antonio Secola asked for a private session with them in which he candidly asked, "Why Michael?"

After a long silence, an old Cardinal took pity on the bewildered man and rose to reply. "We knew you were the better of the two, but we just could not bear the thought of the leader of the Roman Catholic Church being called Pope Secola!"

*   *   *

A young boy had just gotten his driving permit. He asked his father, who was a rabbi, if they could discuss his use of the family car. His father took him into his study and said, "I'll make a deal with you. You bring your grades up, study your

Talmud a little, get your hair cut and then we'll talk about it."

After about a month, the boy came back and again asked his father if they could discuss his use of the car. They again went into the father's study where the father said, "Son, I've been very proud of you. You have brought your grades up, you've studied the Talmud diligently, but you didn't get your hair cut."

The young man waited a moment and then replied, "You know, Dad, I've been thinking about that. You know Samson had long hair, Moses had long hair, Noah had long hair and even Jesus had long hair."

The rabbi said, "Yes, and they walked everywhere they went."

*　　*　　*

Three proofs that Jesus could have been Mexican:
1. His first name was Jesus

2. He was bilingual

3. He was always being harassed by authorities.

But then, there were equally good arguments that:
Jesus could have been black:
1. He called everybody "brother"

2. He liked Gospel

3. He couldn't get a fair trial

And then there were equally good arguments that :

Jesus could have been Jewish:
1. He went into His Father's business
2. He lived at home until He was 33 years old
3. He was sure His mother was a virgin and His mother was sure He was God

But then there were equally good arguments that:
Jesus could have been Italian:
1. He talked with his hands
2. He had wine with every meal
3. He used olive oil

And there were equally good arguments that:
Jesus could have been a Californian:
1. He never cut his hair
2. He walked around barefoot
3. He started a new religion

And of course there were equally good arguments that:
Jesus could have been Irish:
1. He never got married
2. He was always telling stories
3. He loved green pastures

But perhaps the most compelling evidence is that:
Jesus could have been a woman:
1. He had to feed a crowd at a moment's notice when there was no food
2. He kept trying to get a message across to a bunch of men who *just didn't get it*

3. Even when He was dead, He had to get up because there was more work to do!

*   *   *

Irish Alzheimer

Murphy showed up at Mass one Sunday and the priest almost fell down when he saw him. Murphy had never been seen in church in his life. After Mass, the priest caught up with Murphy and said, "Murphy, I am so glad you decided to come to Mass, what made you come?"

Murphy said, "I got to be honest with you Father; a while back, I misplaced me hat and I really, really love that hat. I know that McGlynn had a hat just like me hat and I knew that McGlynn come to church every Sunday. I also knew that McGlynn had to take off his hat during Mass, so I figured he would leave it in the back of church. So, I was going to leave after Communion and steal McGlynn's hat."

The priest said, "Well, Murphy, I notice that you didn't steal McGlynn's hat. What changed your mind?"

Murphy said, "Well, after I heard your sermon on the ten commandments, I decided that I didn't need to steal McGlynn's hat."

The priest gave Murphy a big smile and said, "After I talked about 'Thou Shalt Not Steal' you decided you would rather do without your hat than burn in hell, right?"

Murphy shook his head, and said, "No, Father, after you

talked about 'Thou Shalt Not Commit Adultery' I remember where I left me hat."

          *   *   *

All angels are girls because they gotta wear dresses and boys didn't go for it.
— Antonio, age 9

          *   *   *

For all Catholics who have pondered this philosophical conundrum:

A man wonders if having sex on Sunday is a sin because he is not sure if sex is work or play. So he goes to a priest and asks for his opinion on this question. After consulting the Bible, the priest says, "My son, after our exhaustive search, I am positive that sex is work and is therefore not permitted on Sundays."

The man thinks, "What does a priest know about sex?" So he goes to a Lutheran minister, who after all is a married man and experienced in this matter. He queries the minister and receives the same reply: "Sex is work and therefore not for the Sabbath!"

Not pleased with the reply, he seeks out a rabbi, a man of thousands of years of tradition and knowledge. The rabbi ponders the question, then states, "My son, sex is definitely play."

The man replies, "Rabbi, how can you be so sure when so many others tell me sex is work?" The rabbi softly speaks, "My son, if sex were work, my wife would have the maid do it."

*   *   *

Talking to God

A man was taking it easy, lying on the grass and looking up at the clouds. He was identifying shapes when he decided to talk to God.

"God," he said, "how long is a million years?" God answered, "In my frame of reference, it's about a minute." The man asked, "God, how much is a million dollars?" God answered, "To me, it's a penny." The man then asked, "God, can I have a penny?" God answered, "In a minute."

*   *   *

On their way to get married, a young couple are involved in a fatal car accident. The couple find themselves sitting outside the Pearly Gates waiting for St. Peter to process them into Heaven. While waiting, they begin to wonder: could they possibly get married in Heaven? When St. Peter shows up, they ask him. St. Peter says, "I don't know. This is the first time anyone has asked. Let me go find out," and he leaves.

The couple sat around waiting for an answer for a couple of months. While they waited, they discussed that *if* they were allowed to get married in Heaven, *should* they get married, what with the eternal aspect of it all.

"What if it doesn't work?" They wondered, "Are we stuck together *forever?*"

After yet another month, St. Peter finally returns looking somewhat bedraggled. "Yes, he informs the couple, you *can* get married in Heaven."

"Great!" said the couple, "but we were just wondering, what if things don't work out? Could we also get a divorce in Heaven?"

St. Peter, red-faced with anger, slams his clipboard onto the ground.

"What's wrong?" asked the frightened couple.

"Oh, COME ON!" St. Peter shouts, "It took me three months to find a priest up here! Do you have *any* idea how long it'll take me to find a lawyer?"

*   *   *

When an angel gets mad, he takes a deep breath and counts to ten. And when he lets out his breath, somewhere there's a tornado.

*   *   *

Little Mary Margaret was not the best student in Catholic school. Usually she slept through the class. One day her teacher, a nun, called on her while she was sleeping.

"Tell me, Mary Margaret, who created the universe?" When Mary Margaret didn't stir, little Johnny who was her friend sitting behind her, took his pencil and jabbed her in the rear.

"God Almighty!" shouted Mary Margaret. The nun said, "Very good" and continued teaching her class.

A little later, the nun asked Mary Margaret, "Who is our Lord and Savior?" But Mary didn't stir from her slumber. Once again, Johnny came to her rescue and stuck Mary Margaret in the butt. "Jesus Christ!" shouted Mary Margaret and the nun once again said, "Very good" and Mary Margaret fell back to sleep.

The nun asked her a third question, "What did Eve say to Adam after she had her twenty-third child?"

Again Johnny came to the rescue. This time Mary Margaret jumped up and shouted, "If you stick that damn thing in me once more time, I'll break it in half!"

The nun fainted.

*   *   *

Angels don't eat, but they drink milk from Holy Cows.
— Jack, age 6

*   *   *

Lost on a rainy night, a nun stumbles across a monastery and requests shelter there. Fortunately, she's just in time for dinner and was treated to the best fish and chips she had ever tasted. After dinner, she went into the kitchen to thank the chefs. She was met by two of the Brothers who do the cooking.

The first one said, "Hello, I am Brother Michael, and this is Brother Charles."

"I'm very pleased to meet you," replied the nun. "I just wanted to thank you for a wonderful dinner. The fish and chips were the best I've ever had. Out of curiosity, who cooked what?"

Brother Charles replied, "Well, I'm the fish friar."

She turned to the other Brother and said, "Then you must be...?"

"Yes, I'm afraid so; I'm the chip monk."

*   *   *

The bartender looked over the bar and said, "Here, here, buddy, we won't have any of that carrying on in this bar."

The reverend looked up to the bartender and said, "But you don't understand, I'm Pastor Bush."

The bartender nodded. "Well, if you're that far, you may as well finish!"

*   *   *

What I don't get about angels is why, when someone is in love, they shoot arrows at them.

*   *   *

Church Bulletin

Low Self Esteem Support Group will meet Thursday at 7 p.m. Please use the back door.

*   *   *

As soon as she had finished convent school, a bright young girl named Lena shook the dust of Ireland off her shoes and made her way to New York where before long, she became a successful performer in show business. Eventually she returned to her home town for a visit and on a Sunday night went to confession in the church where she had always attended as a child.

In the confessional, Father Sullivan recognized her and began asking her about her work. She explained that she was an acrobatic dancer, and he wanted to know what that meant. She said she would be happy to show him the kind of thing she did on stage. She stepped out of the confessional and within sight of Father Sullivan, she went into a series of cartwheels, leaping splits, handsprings and back flips.

Kneeling near the confessional, waiting their turn, were two middle-aged ladies. They witnessed Lena's acrobatics with wide eyes, and one said to the other, "Will you jus' look at the penance Father Sullivan is givin' out this night and me without me bloomers on!"

*   *   *

Usually the shop floor staff of the company play football. The middle level managers are more interested in tennis. The top management usually has a preference for golf.

Finding: as you go up the corporate ladder, the balls reduce in size.

*   *   *

Over the massive front doors of a church, these words were inscribed: "The Gate of Heaven". Below that was a small cardboard sign which read: "Please use other entrance."

*   *   *

A driver did the right thing, stopping at the school crosswalk even though he could have beaten the red light by accelerating through the intersection. The tailgating woman behind him went ballistic, pounding on her horn, and screaming in frustration as she missed her chance to drive through the intersection with him. Still in mid-rant, she heard a tap on her window and looked up into the face of a very serious police officer. The officer ordered her to exit her car with her hands up. He took her to the police station where she was searched, fingerprinted, photographed and placed in a cell. After a couple of hours, a policeman approached the cell and opened the door. She was escorted back to the booking desk where the arresting officer was waiting with her personal effects.

He said, "I'm awfully sorry for this mistake. You see, I pulled up behind your car while you were blowing your horn, flipping the guy off in front of you, and cussing a blue streak at him. That was when I noticed the 'What Would Jesus Do' license plate holder, the 'Follow me to Sunday School' bumper sticker, the chrome plated Christian fish emblem on the trunk and the 'My Boss is a Jewish Carpenter' decal on your back window.

Naturally, I assumed you had stolen the car."

*   *   *   *   *

Death Reflections

When you are in your casket and friends, family and congregants are mourning over you, what would you like to hear them say?

Episcopal priest says, "I would like to hear them say that I was a wonderful husband, a fine spiritual leader, and a great family man."

Catholic priest says: "I would like to hear that I was a wonderful teacher and a servant of God who made a huge difference in people's lives."

The rabbi says: "I would like to hear them say, 'Look, he's alive!'"

*   *   *

Old Fred's hospital bed is surrounded by well wishers, but it doesn't look good. Suddenly he motions frantically to the pastor for something to write on. The pastor lovingly hands him a pen and a piece of paper and Fred uses his last bit of energy to scribble a note, and dies.

The pastor thinks it best not to look at the note right away, so he places it in his jacket pocket. At Fred's funeral, as the pastor is finishing his eulogy, he realizes he's wearing the jacket he was wearing when Fred died.

"Fred handed me a note just before he died," he says, "I haven't looked at it but knowing Fred, I'm sure there's a word of inspiration in it for us all."

Open the note, he reads aloud, "Help! You're standing on my oxygen tube!"

*   *   *

A man was just waking up from anesthesia after surgery and his wife was sitting by his side. His eyes fluttered open and he said, "You're beautiful." Then he fell asleep again. His wife had never heard him say that, so she stayed by his side.

A few minutes later, his eyes fluttered open and he said, "You're cute!"

The wife was disappointed because instead of "beautiful" it was now "cute". She said, "What happened to 'beautiful'?" The man replied, "The drugs are wearing off!"

* * *

The new priest is nervous about hearing confessions, so he asks an older priest to sit in on his sessions. The new priest hears a couple of confessions, then the old priest asks him to step out of the confessional for a few suggestions.

The old priest suggest, "Cross your arms over your chest and rub your chin with one hand." The new priest tries this.

The old priest suggests, "Try saying things like, 'I see,' 'yes,' 'go on,' 'I understand,' and 'how did you feel about that?'" The new priest says those things, trying them out.

The old priest says, "Now, don't you think that's a little better than slapping your knee and saying 'No shit! What happened next?'"

* * *

A woman went to the post office to buy stamps for her Christmas cards. "What denomination?" asked the clerk. "Oh, good heavens! Have we come to this?" said the woman. "Well, give me 50 Baptist and 50 Catholic ones."

* * *

In 2030 Bill Gates died in a car accident. He found himself in Purgatory being sized up by God. "Well, Bill, I'm really confused on this call," God said. "I'm not sure whether to send you to heaven or hell. After all, you helped society enormously by putting a computer in almost every home in the world and yet you created that ghastly Windows Vista. I'm going to do something I've never done before. In your case, I'm going to let you decide where you want to go!"

Bill replied, "Well, thanks, God. What's the difference between the two?"
God said, "I'm willing to let you visit both places briefly if it will help you make a decision."
"Fine, but where should I go first?"
God said, "I'm going to leave that you to you."
Bill said, "OK, then let's try hell first."

So Bill went to hell. It was beautiful with clean, sandy beaches and clear waters. There were thousands of beautiful women running around, playing in the water, laughing and frolicking about. The sun was shining. The temperature was perfect. Bill was very pleased.

"This is great", he told God. "If this is hell, I really want to see heaven!"
"Fine," said God, and off they went. Heaven was a high place in the clouds with angels drifting about playing harps and singing. It was nice but not as enticing as hell. Bill thought for a quick minutes and rendered his decision.
"Hmmm, I think I prefer hell," he told God. "Fine," retorted God, "as you desire." So Bill Gates went to hell.

Two weeks later, God decided to check up on the late billionaire to see how he was doing in hell. When God arrived in hell, he found Bill shackled to a wall, screaming among the hot flames in a dark cave. He was being burned and tortured by demons.

"How's everything going, Bill?" God asked. Bill, his voice full of anguish and disappointment, responded, "This is awful. This is not what I expected. I can't believe it. What happened to that other place with the beaches and the beautiful women playing in the water?"

God smiled and said, "That was the screen saver."

*   *   *

Rev. Warren J. Keating, Pastor of the First Presbyterian Church of Yuma, AZ, says that the best prayer he ever heard was: "Lord, please make me the kind of person my dog thinks I am."

*   *   *

Father O'Malley got up one fine spring day and walked to the window of his bedroom to get a deep breath of the beautiful day outside and noticed there was a jackass lying dead in the middle of his front lawn. He promptly called the local police station. The conversation went like this:

"Top o' the day to ye. This is Sgt. Flaherty. How might I help ye?"

"And the rest of the day te yerself. This is Father O'Malley at St. Brigit's. There's a jackass lying dead in me front lawn. Would ye be after sending a couple o' yer lads to take care of the matter?"

Now Sgt. Flaherty considered himself to be quite a wit and the rest of the conversation proceeded:

"Well, now Father, it was always my impression that you people took care of last rites!"

There was dead silence on the line for a moment and then Father O'Malley replied: "Aye, that's certainly true but we are also obliged to notify the next of kin!"

*   *   *

Church Bulletin
Barbara remains in the hospital and needs blood donors for more transfusions. She is also having trouble sleeping and requests tapes of Pastor Jack's sermons.

*   *   *

The Robe

Jesus is wandering around Jerusalem when he decides he really needs a new robe. After looking around, he sees a sign for 'Finkelstein, the Tailor.' He goes in and Finkelstein prepares a new robe for him, which is a perfect fit. When he asks how much he owes, Finkelstein brushes him off:

"No, no, no, for the Son of God? There's no charge. However, may I ask a small favor? Maybe whenever you give a sermon you could just mention a little something about how your nice new robe was made by Finkelstein the Tailor."

Jesus readily agrees and, as promised, plugs Finkelstein's robes every time he preaches. Some months later, Jesus is walking through Jerusalem and happens by Finkelstein's shop. There is a huge line of people waiting for Finkelstein's robes. He pushes his way through the crowd to speak to Finkelstein.

"Jesus, Jesus, look what a marvel you've been for business!" gushed Finkelstein. "Would you consider a partnership?"

"Sure, sure," replies Jesus. "Jesus & Finkelstein it is."

"Oh, no, no", says Finkelstein. "Finkelstein & Jesus. After all, I am the craftsman."

The two of them debated this for some time. Their discussion was long and spirited, but ultimately fruitful. Finally, they came up with a mutually acceptable compromise. A few days later, the new sign went up over Finkelstein's shop: 'Lord & Tailor'

$$*\qquad*\qquad*$$

Pastor Dave Charlton tells us, "After a worship service at First Baptist Church in Newcastle, Kentucky, a mother with a fidgety seven-year-old boy told me how she finally got her son to sit still and be quiet. About halfway through the sermon, she leaned over and whispered, 'If you don't be quiet, Pastor Charlton is going to lose his place and will have to start his sermon all over again!' It worked."

$$*\qquad*\qquad*$$

A guy just died and he's at the Pearly Gates, waiting to be admitted, while St. Peter is leafing through this Big Book to see if the guy is worthy. St. Peter goes through the Book several times, furrows his brow and says to the guy, "You know, I can't see that you ever did anything really bad in your life but you never did anything really good either. If you can point to even one *really good deed* — you're in."

The guy thinks for a moment and says, "Yeah, there was this one time when I was driving down the highway and saw a giant group of thugs assaulting this poor girl. I slowed down my car to see what was going on and sure enough, there they were, about fifty of them harassing this terrified young woman."

"Infuriated, I got out of my car, grabbed a tire iron out of my trunk, and walked up to the leader of the gang, a huge guy with a studded leather jacket and a chain running from his nose to his ear. As I walked up to the leader, the thugs formed a circle around me. So, I ripped the leader's chain off his face and smashed him over the head with the tire iron. Laid him out. Then I turned and yelled at the rest of them, "Leave this poor innocent girl alone! You're all a bunch of sick, deranged animals! Go home before I teach you all a lesson in pain!"

St. Peter, impressed, says, "Really? When did this happen?"

"Oh, about two minutes ago."

*   *   *

Don't Step on a Duck

Three guys die together in an accident and go to heaven. When they get there, St. Peter says, "We only have one rule here in heaven: don't step on the ducks."

So they enter heaven, and sure enough, there are ducks all over the place. It is almost impossible not to step on a duck, and although they try their best to avoid them, the first guy accidentally steps on one.

Along comes St. Peter with the ugliest woman he ever saw. St. Peter chains them together and says, "Your punishment for stepping on a duck is to spend eternity chained to this ugly woman!"

The next day, the second guy steps accidentally on a duck, and along comes St. Peter, who doesn't miss a thing, and with him is another extremely ugly woman. He chains them together with the same admonishment as for the first guy.

The third guy has observed all this and not wanting to be chained for all eternity to an ugly woman, is very, *very* careful where he steps. He manages to go months without stepping on any ducks, but one day St. Peter comes up to him with the most gorgeous woman he has ever laid eyes on — a very tall, tan, curvaceous, sexy blonde. St. Peter chains them together without saying a word.

The guy remarks, "I wonder what I did to deserve being chained to you for all of eternity?"

She says, "I don't know about you, but I stepped on a duck."

*   *   *

As a new bride, Aunt Edna moved into the small home on her husband's ranch near Snowflake. She put a shoe box on a shelf in her closet and asked her husband never to touch it.

For fifty years, Uncle Jack left the box alone, until Aunt Edna was old and dying. One day when he was putting their affairs in order, he found the box again and thought it might hold something important.

Opening it, he found two doilies and $82,500 in cash. He took the box to her and asked about the contents.

"My mother gave me that box the day we married," she explained. "She told me to make a doily to help ease my frustrations every time I got mad at you."

Uncle Jack was very touched that in fifty years, she'd been mad at him only twice.

"What's the $82,500?" he asked. "Oh, well, that's the money I've made selling the doilies."

*   *   *

A minister decided to do something a little different one Sunday morning. He said, "Today, church, I am going to say a single word and you are going to help me preach. Whatever single word I say, I want you to sing whatever hymn that comes to your mind."

The pastor shouted out, "Cross." Immediately the congregation started singing in unison "The Old Rugged Cross."

The pastor hollered out "Grace." The congregation began to sing "Amazing Grace, how sweet the sound."

The pastor said "Power." The congregation sang "There is Power in the Blood."

The pastor said "Sex." The congregation fell in total silence. Everyone was in shock. They all nervously began to look around at each other afraid to say anything.

Then all of a sudden, from way in the back of the church a little old 87-year-old grandmother stood up and began to sing "Precious Memories."

*   *   *

The Smile

There once was a religious young woman who went to confession. Upon entering the confessional she said, "Forgive me, Father, for I have sinned." The priest said, "Confess your sins and be forgiven."

The young woman said, "Last night my boyfriend made mad passionate love to me seven times." The priest thought long and hard and then said, "Squeeze seven lemons into a glass and then drink the juice."

The young woman said, "Will this cleanse me of my sins?" The priest said, "No, but it will wipe that smile off of your face."

*   *   *

The elder priest, speaking to the younger priest, said, "I know you were reaching out to the young people of the parish when you installed bucket seats to replace the first four pews. And it worked very well. We got the front of the church filled first."

The young priest nodded and the old one continued, "And,

you told me a little more beat to the music would bring young people back to church, so I supported you when you brought in that rock and roll gospel choir that packed our little church all the way to the balcony."

"So," asked the young priest, "what's the problem?" "Well", said the elder priest, "I'm afraid you've gone too far with the drive-thru confessional."

"But, Father," protests the young priest, "My confessions have nearly doubled since I began that!" "I know, I know, my son, but the flashing neon sign 'TOOT 'N' TELL OR GO TO HELL' really has to go!"

*   *   *

Church Bulletin

A bean supper will be held on Tuesday evening in the church hall. Music will follow.

*   *   *

An atheist was taking a walk through the woods, admiring all that the 'accident of evolution' had created. "What majestic trees! What powerful rivers! What beautiful animals!" he said to himself.

As he was walking alongside the river he heard a rustling in the bushes behind. As he turned to look, he saw a 7-foot grizzly bear charge towards him. He ran as fast as he could up the path. He looked over his shoulder and saw that the bear was closing in on him. He tried to run even faster, so scared that tears were coming to his eyes. He looked over his shoulder again and the bear was even closer. His heart was pumping frantically as he tried to run even faster, but he tripped and fell on the ground.

He rolled over to pick himself up and saw the bear right on top of him raising his paw to kill him. At that instant, he cried out, "Oh, my God!". Just then, time stopped. The bear froze, the forest was silent, and the river even stopped moving. A bright light shone upon the man, and a voice came out of the sky, saying, "You deny my existence all of these years, teach others I don't exist and even credit my creation to a cosmic accident and now , do you expect me to help you out of this predicament? Am I to count you as a believer?"

The atheist, ever so proud, looked into the light and said, "It would be rather hypocritical to ask to be a Christian after all these years, but could you make the bear a Christian?"

"Very well," said the voice. The light went out, the river ran, the sounds of the forest continued and the bear put his paw down. The bear then brought both paws together, bowed his head and said, "Lord, I thank you for this food which I am about to receive."

*   *   *

A drunken bloke staggers into a Catholic church and sits down in the confessional box and says nothing. The bewildered priest coughs to attract attention, but still the man says nothing. The priest then knocks on the wall three times in a final attempt to get the man to speak. Finally the drunk replies, "No use knockin', mate, there's no paper in this one either!"

*   *   *

There was a Scottish tradesman, a painter called Jock, who

was very interested in making a pound where he could, so he often would thin down his paint to make it go a wee bit further.

As it happened, he got away with this for some time but eventually the Presbyterian Church decided to do a big restoration job on the roof of one of their biggest churches. Jock put in a bid and because his price was so competitive, he got the job.

And so he set to, with a right good will, erecting the trestles and putting up the planks, and buying the paint and yes, I am sorry to say, thinning it down with the turpentine.

Well, Jock was up on the scaffolding, painting away, the job nearly done, when suddenly there was a horrendous clap of thunder and the sky opened up, the rain poured down, washing the thin paint from all over the church, knocking Jock fair off the scaffold to land on the lawn, among the gravestones, surrounded by telltale puddles of the thinned and useless paint.

Jock was no fool. He knew this was a judgment from the Almighty, so he fell on his knees and cried out, "Oh, God! Forgive me! What should I do?"

And from the thunder, a might Voice spoke, "Repaint and thin no more!"

*   *   *

Church Bulletin

Don't let worry kill you off — let the Church help.

*   *   *

A local priest and pastor were fishing on the side of the road. They thoughtfully made a sign saying, "The End is Near! Turn yourself around now before it's too late!" and showed it to each passing car.

One driver that drove by didn't appreciate the sign and shouted at them, "Leave us alone, you religious nuts!"

All of a sudden they heard a big splash, looked at each other and the priest said to the pastor, "Do you think we should just put up a sign that says 'BRIDGE OUT' instead?"

*   *   *

How old would you be if you didn't know how old you are?

*   *   *

A Pot of Potent Beans

One of the matrons of the church was cooking a pot of her famous beans for the church potluck and her son, little Johnny, came running through the house, BB gun in one hand and a handful of BBs in the other. He tripped and the BBs, naturally, went right into the pot of beans. Thinking it over, little Johnny could think of no reason why he should risk punishment, so he said nothing.

The dinner went well, and as usual the beans were one of the favorite dishes. The next day, the church secretary, Mary, called little Johnny's mother and said, "Jane, your beans were delicious as usual, but what did you put in them this time?"

Jane replied, "Nothing new, why do you ask?"

"Well," said Mary, "this morning I bent over to feed the cat and I shot the canary!"

*   *   *

Church Bulletin

At the evening service tonight, the sermon topic will be 'What is Hell?' Come early and listen to our choir practice.

*   *   *

God and Eve in the Garden of Eden

One day in the Garden of Eden, Eve calls out to God, "Lord, I have a problem!"

"What's the problem, Eve?"

"Lord, I know you created me and provided this beautiful garden and all of these wonderful animals and that hilarious snake, but I'm just not happy."

"Why is that, Eve?" came the reply from above.

"Lord, I am lonely, and I'm sick to death of apples."

"Well, Eve, in that case, I have a solution. I shall create a man for you."

"What's a man, Lord?"

"This man will be a flawed creature, with many bad traits. He'll lie, cheat, and be vain; all in all, he'll give you a hard time. But, he'll be bigger, faster, and will like to hunt and kill things. He will look silly when he's aroused, but since you've been complaining, I'll create him in such a way that he will satisfy your physical needs. He will be witless and will revel in childish things like fighting and kicking a ball about. He won't be too smart, so he'll also need your advice to think properly."

"Sounds great," says Eve, with an ironically raised eyebrow. "What's the catch, Lord?"

"Well… you can have him on one condition."

"What's that, Lord?"

"As I said, he'll be proud, arrogant, and self-admiring; so you'll have to let him believe that I made him first. Just remember, it's our little secret — you know, woman to woman."

*   *   *

Two Irishmen were sitting in a pub having beer and watching the brothel across the street. They saw a Baptist minister walk into the brothel, and one of them said, "Aye, 'tis a shame to see a man of the cloth goin' bad."

Then they saw a rabbi enter the brothel, and the other Irishman said, "Aye, 'tis a shame to see that the Jews are fallin' victim to temptation."

Then they saw a Catholic priest enter the brothel, and one of the Irishmen said, "What a terrible pity - one of the girls must be quite ill."

* * *

Crossword Puzzle

One day, a shy gentleman was preparing to board a plane when he heard that the Pope was on the same flight.

"This is exciting," thought the gentleman. "I've always been a big fan of the Pope. Perhaps I'll be able to see him in person." Suddenly, the man realized his seat was right next to the Pope himself. Still, the gentleman was too shy to speak to the Pope. Shortly after take-off, the Pope took a crossword puzzle out of his bag and began working on it.

"This is fantastic," thought the gentleman. "I'm really good at crosswords. Perhaps if the Pope gets stuck, he'll ask me for assistance." Almost immediately, the Pope turned to the man and said, "Excuse me, but do you know a four letter word referring to a woman that ends in 'unt'"?

The man was in shock. He could only think of one word that fit that description and he was not about to say it to the Pope. The gentleman thought for a while longer, then it hit him.

Turning to the Pope, the gentleman said, "I think you're look for the word 'aunt'."

* * *

Religious Philosophies of the World in a Nutshell

Catholicism:	If shit happens, I deserve it.
Protestantism:	Shit won't happen if I work harder.
Judaism:	Why does this shit always happen to me?
Buddhism:	When shit happens, is it really shit?

Islam:	If shit happens, take a hostage.
Hinduism:	This shit happened before.
Hare Krishna:	Shit happens, Rama Lama Ding Dong.
Rastafarian:	Let's smoke this shit.

* * *

Church Bulletin

The senior choir invites any member of the congregation who enjoys sinning to join the choir.

* * *

Sarah, the church gossip and self-appointed supervisor of the church's morals, kept sticking her nose into other people's business. Several members were unappreciative of her activities, but feared her enough to maintain their silence.

She made a mistake, however, when she accused George, a new member, of being an alcoholic after she saw his pickup truck parked in front of the town's only bar one afternoon. She commented to George and others that everyone seeing it there would know that he was an alcoholic.

George, a man of few words, stared at her for a moment and just walked away. He said nothing.

Later that evening, George quietly parked his pickup in front of Sarah's house and he left it there all night.

* * *

Church Bulletin

Ladies, don't forget the rummage sale. It's a chance to get rid of those things not worth keeping around the house. Don't forget your husbands.

*   *   *

John Smith was the only Protestant to move into a large Catholic neighborhood. On the first Friday of Lent, John was outside grilling a nice juicy steak on his grill. Meanwhile, all of his neighbors were eating cold tuna fish for supper. This went on each Friday of Lent.

On the last Friday of Lent, the neighborhood men got together and decided that something had to be done about John; he was tempting them to eat meat each Friday of Lent and they couldn't take it anymore. They decided to try to convert John to be a Catholic. They went over and talked to him and were so happy that he decided to join all of his neighbors and become a Catholic.

They took him to church and the priest sprinkled some water over him and said, "You were born a Baptist, you were raised a Baptist, and now you are a Catholic."

The men were so relieved now that their biggest Lenten temptation was resolved. The next year's Lenten season rolled around. The first Friday of Lent came and just at supper time, when the neighborhood was sitting down to their cold tuna fish dinner, came the wafting smell of steak cooking on a grill. The neighborhood men could not believe their noses!

What was going on? They called each other up and decided to meet over in John's yard to see if he had forgotten it was the first Friday of Lent. The group arrived just in time to see John standing over his grill with a small pitcher of water. He was sprinkling some water over his steak on the grill, saying,

"You were born a cow, you were raised a cow, and now you are a fish."

*   *   *

Two cannibals meet one day. The first cannibal says, "You know, I just can't seem to get a tender missionary. I've baked them, I've stewed them, I've roasted them, and I've barbecued them — I just cannot seem to get them tender."

The second cannibal asks, "What kind of missionary do you use?"
The other replied, "You know, they have those brown cloaks with a rope around the waist and they're sort of bald on top with a funny ring of hair on their heads."

"Ah, that's it!" the second cannibal replies. "No wonder - those are friars!"

*   *   *

A drunk man who smelled like liquor sat down on a subway seat next to a priest. The man's tie was stained, his face was plastered with red lipstick, and a half empty bottle of gin was sticking out of his torn coat pocket. He opened his newspaper and began reading. After a few minutes the man turned to the priest and asked, "Say, Father, what causes arthritis?"

"My son, it's caused by loose living, being with cheap, wicked women, too much alcohol and contempt for your fellow man, sleeping around with prostitutes and lack of bathing."

"Well, I'll be damned," the drunk muttered, returning to his paper.

The priest, thinking about what he had said, nudged the man and apologized.

"I'm very sorry. I didn't mean to come on so strong. How long have you had arthritis?"

"I don't have it, Father. I was just reading here that the Pope does."

*   *   *

After being nearly snowbound for two weeks last winter, a Seattle man departed for his vacation in Miami Beach, where he was to meet his wife the next day at the conclusion of her business trip to Minneapolis. They were looking forward to pleasant weather and a nice time together. Unfortunately, there was some sort of mix up at the boarding gate, and the man was told he would have to wait for a later flight. He tried to appeal to a supervisor but was told the airline was not responsible for the problem and it would do no good to complain.

Upon arrival at the hotel the next day, he discovered that Miami Beach was having a heat wave, and its weather was almost as uncomfortably hot as Seattle's was cold. The desk clerk gave him a message that his wife would arrive as planned. He could hardly wait to get to the pool area to cool off, and quickly sent his wife an email, but due to his haste, he made an error in the email address. His message therefore arrived at the home of an elderly preacher's wife whose even older husband had died only the day before.

When the grieving widow opened her email, she took one

look at the monitor, let out an anguished scream, and fell to the floor dead. Her family rushed to her room where they saw this message on the screen:

Dearest wife, Departed yesterday as you know. Just now got checked in. Some confusion at the gate. Appeal was denied. Received confirmation of your arrival tomorrow.

Your loving husband.
P.S. Things are not as we thought. You're going to be surprised at how hot it is down here.

*   *   *

Church Bulletin
Bertha Belch, a missionary from Africa will be speaking tonight at Calvary Memorial Church in Racine. Come tonight and hear Bertha Belch all the way from Africa.

*   *   *

Miss Bea, the church organist, was in her eighties and had never been married. She was much admired for her sweetness and kindness to all.

The pastor came to call on her one afternoon early in the spring, and she welcomed him into her Victorian parlor. She invited him to have a seat while she prepared a little tea. As he sat facing her old pump organ, the young minister noticed a cut glass bowl sitting on top of it, filled with water. In the water floated, of all things, a condom. Imagine his shock and surprise. Imagine his curiosity. Surely Miss Bea had flipped or something!

When she returned with tea and cookies, they began to chat.

The pastor tried to stifle his curiosity about the bowl of water and its strange floater, but soon it got the better of him and he could resist no longer.

"Miss Bea," he said, "I wonder if you would tell me about this?", pointing to the bowl.

"Oh, yes," she replied, "Isn't it wonderful? I was walking downtown last fall and I found this little package on the ground. The directions said to put it on the organ, keep it wet, and it would prevent disease. And you know, I haven't had a single cold all winter."

*   *   *

"What is this?" Alex asked.
"Well, son, it's a memorial to all the young men and women who died in the service."
Soberly, they stood together, staring at the large plaque.
Little Alex's voice was trembling and barely audible when he asked, "Which service, the 9:45 or the 11:15?"

*   *   *

In Jerusalem, an American female journalist heard about an old rabbi who visited the Wailing Wall to pray, twice a day, every day for a long, long time.

In an effort to check out the story, she went to the holy site and there he was. She watched the bearded old man at prayer, and after about 45 minutes, when he turned to leave, she approached him for an interview.

"I'm Rebecca Smith from CNN, sir. How long have you been coming to the Wailing Wall and praying?"

"For about 50 years," he informed her. "Fifty years! That's amazing. What do you pray for?"

"I pray for peace between the Jews and the Arabs. I pray for all the hatred to stop and I pray for all our children to grow up in safety and friendship."

"And how do you feel, sir, after doing this for 50 years?"

"Like I'm talking to a fucking wall."

*   *   *

"Do you believe in life after death?" the boss asked one of his employees.
"Yes, sir," the new employee replied.
"Well, then, that makes everything just fine," the boss went on. "After you left early yesterday to go to your grandmother's funeral, she stopped in to see you."

*   *   *

Dead Sea Scroll

A team of archaeologists was excavating in Israel when they came upon a cave. Written across the wall of the cave were the following symbols:

It was considered a unique find and the writings were said to be at least three thousand years old! The piece of stone was removed, brought to the museum and archaeologists from around the world came to study the ancient symbols. They held a huge meeting after months of conferences to discuss the meaning of the markings.

The president of the society pointed to the first drawing and said, "This is a woman. We can see these people held women in high esteem. You can also tell they were intelligent, as the next symbol is a donkey, so they were smart enough to have animals help them till the soil. The next drawing is a shovel, which means they had tools to help them. Even further proof of their high intelligence is the fish which means that if a famine hit the earth and food didn't grow, they sought food from the sea. The last symbol appears to be the Star of David, which means they were evidently Hebrews."

The audience applauded enthusiastically.

Then a little old Jewish man stood up in the back of the room and said, "Idiots, Hebrew is read from *RIGHT* to *LEFT*. It says:

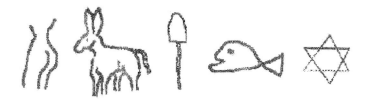

'Holy Mackerel Dig the Ass on that Woman'".

* * *

Pastor's Business Card
A new pastor was visiting in the homes of his parishioners. At one house it seemed obvious that someone was at home, but no answer came to his repeated knocks at the door. Therefore, he took out a business card and wrote 'Revelation 3:20' on the back of it and stuck it in the door.

When the offering was processed the following Sunday, he found that his card had been returned. Added to it was this cryptic message, 'Genesis 3:10.'

Reaching for his Bible to check out the citation, he broke up in gales of laughter. Revelation 3:20 begins 'Behold, I stand at the door and knock.' Genesis 3:10 reads, 'I heard your voice in the garden and I was afraid for I was naked.'

* * *

An Amish boy and his father were in a mall. They were amazed by almost everything they saw, but especially by two shiny, silver walls that could move apart and then slide back together again.

The boy asked, "What is this, Father?" The father (never

having seen an elevator) responded, "Son, I have never seen anything like this in my life; I don't know what it is."

While the boy and his father were watching with amazement, a fat old lady in a wheel chair moved up to the moving walls and pressed a button. The walls opened, and the lady rolled between them into a small room. The walls closed, and the boy and his father watched the small numbers above the walls light up sequentially. They continued to watch until it reached the last number, and then the numbers began to light in the reverse order. Finally the walls opened up again and a gorgeous 24-year-old blonde stepped out.

The father, not taking his eyes off the young woman, said quietly to his son, "Go get your mother."

*   *   *

A distinguished looking young woman on a flight from Ireland asked the priest beside her, "Father, may I ask a favor?"
"Of course, child. What may I do for you?"
"Well, I bought an expensive woman's electronic hair dryer for my mother's birthday that is unopened and well over the Customs' limits, and I'm afraid they'll confiscate it. Is there any way you could carry it through customs for me? Under your robes perhaps?"
"I would love to help you, dear, but I must warn you: I will not lie."
"With your honest face, Father, no one will question you."

When they got to Customs, she let the priest go ahead of her. The official asked, "Father, do you have anything to declare?"

"From the top of my head down to my waist, I have nothing to declare."

The official thought this answer was strange, so he asked, "And what do you have to declare from your waist to the floor?"

"I have a marvelous instrument designed to be used on a woman, but which is, to date, unused."

Roaring with laughter, the official said, "Go ahead, Father...... Next!"

*   *   *

Two Jehovah's Witnesses die and go to heaven. As they are standing patiently outside the Pearly Gates, they hear a voice inside whisper

"Turn out the lights and everybody be quiet. Maybe they'll think we aren't home."

*   *   *

While on vacation in Rome, I noticed a marble column in St. Peter's with a golden telephone on it. As a young priest passed by, I asked who the telephone was for. The priest told me it was a direct line to heaven, and if I'd like to call, it would be a thousand dollars. I was amazed, but declined the offer. Throughout Italy, I kept seeing the same golden telephone on a marble column. At each, I asked about it and the answer was always the same: It was a direct line to heaven and I could call for a thousand dollars.

When - I finished my tour in Ireland, I decided to attend Mass at a local village church. When I walked in the door I noticed the golden telephone. Underneath it, there was a sign stating:

"DIRECT LINE TO HEAVEN: 25 cents."

"Father," I said, "I have been all over Italy and in all the cathedrals I visited, I've seen telephones exactly like this one. But the price is always a thousand dollars. Why is it that this one is only 25 cents?"

The priest smiled and said, "My son, you're in Ireland now. It's a local call."

*　　*　　*

Shirley and Marcy

A mom was concerned about her kindergarten son walking to school. He didn't want his mother to walk with him. She wanted to give him the feeling that he had some independence but yet know that he was safe. So she had an idea of how to handle it. She asked a neighbor if she would please follow him to school in the mornings, staying a distance, so he probably wouldn't notice her.

The neighbor said that since she was up early with her toddler anyway, it would be a good way for them to get some exercise as well, so she agreed.

The next school day, the neighbor and her little girl set out following behind Timmy as he walked to school with another neighbor girl he knew. She did this for the whole week.

As the two walked and chatted, kicking stones and twigs, Timmy's little friend noticed that the same lady was following them, as she had every day.

Finally she said to Timmy, "Have you noticed that lady following us to school all week? Do you know her?"
Timmy nonchalantly replied, "Yeah, I know who she is."
The little girl said, "Well, who is she?"

"That's just Shirley Goodnest," Timmy replied, "and her daughter Marcy."
"Shirley Goodnest? Who is she and why is she following us?"
"Well," Timmy explained, "every night my Mom makes me say the 23rd Psalm with my prayers, 'cuz she worries about me so much. And in the Psalm, it says, 'Shirley Goodnest and Marcy shall follow me all the days of my life', so I guess I'll just have to get used to it!:

*   *   *

More 'Said by children'
Give us this steak and daily bread, and forgive us our mattresses.

Hail Mary, full of grapes.

Our Father, who art in Heaven, how didja know my name?

Give us this day our jelly bread.

He suffered under a bunch of violets. ('under Pontius Pilate')

Lead a snot into temptation.   (get your sister in trouble?)

*   *   *

When my older brother was very young, he always walked up to the church altar with my mother when she took communion.

On one occasion, he tugged at her arm and asked, "What does the priest say when he gives you the bread?" Mom whispered something in his ear. Imagine his shock many years later when he learned that the priest doesn't say, "Be quiet until you get to your seat."

*   *   *